the 9

BEST PRACTICES FOR YOUTH MINISTRY

KURT JOHNSTON
TIM LEVERT

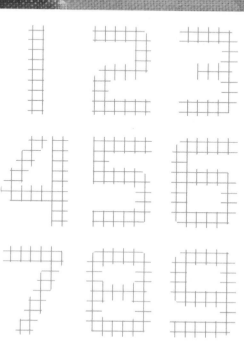

The 9: Best Practices for Youth Ministry
Kurt Johnston & Tim Levert

group.com
simplyyouthministry.com

Credits
Authors: Kurt Johnston & Tim Levert
Executive Developer: Nadim Najm
Chief Creative Officer: Joani Schultz
Editor: Nancy Going and Rick Lawrence
Copy Editor: Rob Cunningham
Cover Art and Production: Veronica Lucas
Production Manager: DeAnne Lear

Library of Congress Cataloging-in-Publication Data
Johnston, Kurt, 1966-
The 9 : best practices for youth ministry / Kurt Johnston and Tim Levert.
    p. cm.
  ISBN 978-0-7644-4134-9 (pbk. : alk. paper)
  1. Church group work with youth. I. Levert, Tim, 1972- II. Title.
III. Title: Nine.
  BV4447.J53 2010
  259'.23--dc22   2010022198

ISBN 978-0-7644-4134-9

10 9 8 7 6 5 4 3 2 1   18 17 16 15 14 13 12 11 10

Printed in the United States of America.

DEDICATION

We would like to dedicate this book to the men who gave us our first "shot" at youth ministry. We were both hired at young ages by senior pastors who believed in the importance of student ministry and were convinced we could help their churches do it well.

Thank you Pastor Ronald L. Prinzing from First Family Church in Whittier, California, for seeing something in me that made you take such a bold risk! I am eternally grateful.

- Kurt Johnston

Thank you Willis Ray Curtis and Glen Whatley for giving me a chance to re-experience God's love by serving in ministry. I love you guys.

- Tim Levert

Acknowledgments

We want to thank our wonderful wives, Rachel Johnston and Tasha Levert, for allowing us the freedom to undertake this project. As usual, your sacrifices were far greater than ours. We would like to thank Mark Eades, Rick Lawrence, and Nancy Going for taking the time to read this manuscript and lend valuable insight. We would like to thank Luther Seminary and the good folks from the Exemplary Youth Ministries study for trusting us with their research and for extending grace where we botched your hard work! We would like to extend an extra measure of thanks to Dr. Wes Black from Southwestern Baptist Theological Seminary for giving us a hands-on, insider's look at the EYM study. And we want to thank all youth workers who are living and revealing the kingdom of God with their students.

TABLE OF CONTENTS

INTRODUCTION

In the summer of 1999, I (Kurt) spoke at a youth summer camp in
Soldotna, Alaska, and met a youth worker and worship leader named
Tim. Because we didn't have a ton of other responsibilities, we often
found ourselves killing time by avoiding moose nuggets, playing golf
at midnight under sunny skies, and wondering where all the Eskimos
and igloos were. Tim and I stayed in touch, and we often found our
conversations revolving around important youth ministry questions like:

- What brand of toilet paper is the toughest to remove from
  our trees?
- What is the truth behind the disappearance of
  Chubby Bunny?
- What are the chemical elements that make the "blue
  flame" blue?

Occasionally we would stumble upon more meaningful questions that
you and your youth ministry friends are probably discussing:

- Is what we're doing making a difference?
- How can I know if I'm doing the right stuff?
- Does healthy youth ministry really exist?
- Does youth ministry need to be totally deconstructed?
- Is there a role for youth ministry in the future of the church?

This book is a continuation of our conversation and an invitation for you to join us on our journey.

One of the questions that we've all heard asked in recent years is, "Why do so many teenagers drop out of church when they graduate from high school?" A group of very smart people who do a lot of thinking about youth ministry decided to spend some time researching this question. In a nutshell, they found that students who dropped out of church didn't have a mature faith in Christ. (We know, we know, not very surprising. It gets better.) As we read through their findings and compared notes from our own conversations, we began asking additional questions: "What practices can we adopt that create an environment that will give students the things they need to have mature faith in Christ?" and "Are there some 'best practices' of student ministry that will help develop mature faith in our teenagers' lives? The short answer is, "Yes!" If you're good with that, please skip the next paragraph; if you want the long answer, keep reading; if you're bored with the intro, feel free to turn to chapter one and get started.

It will come as no surprise that mature faith doesn't magically appear just because a youth leader shows up on Sunday evenings with pizza and a Bible. Helping students become this type of maturing person is the result of intentionality on the part of those of us who lead ministry. The very smart people we mentioned earlier conducted a research project entitled the Study of Exemplary Congregations in Youth Ministry (from now on, we'll refer to this study as EYM; see Appendix for more info). The EYM study identified youth ministries nationwide that were successful in graduating students with mature Christian faith. As researchers studied these church communities more closely, they identified eight practices common to these "exemplary congregations." Recognizing that many youth leaders don't want to plow through academic research (because we'd rather play video games or see how many Twinkies® we can eat in 60 seconds) we've dedicated this book to unpacking these eight practices in simple language and exploring how to implement them in our ministries.

One small point of confession: We fudged a bit. After poring through the research data and the results (which, by the way, Tim pored through repeatedly; Kurt, not so much…Twinkies®), we added a ninth practice that emphasizes the spiritual health of the leader. We believe the spiritual health of the leader is the most important "best practice" you can adopt, so you'll find that conversation in chapter one. In the following eight chapters, we explore the eight practices in no particular order—except for the last chapter, which we're inclined to believe is the least important. You'll just have to wait and see what that one is. (Who are we kidding; you're probably flipping back there right now to see which one is least important.)

Allow us to share a few assumptions that will help you understand our starting point:

> 1. We are targeting students' spiritual health, not traditional markers of growth. We want to measure the health of youth ministry not by weekly attendance, but by longer-range effectiveness of shaping teenagers toward genuine faith

maturity. We hope this difference relieves some pressure from you—and adds a healthier sort of pressure.

2. We're not arguing that youth ministry is broken. In fact, we generally disagree with the books and articles claiming that it is. Many of you are already doing good stuff. Keep doing it! Hold on to what you're doing well. We believe tons of churches around the world are doing good, healthy youth ministry. We are only encouraging you (and us) to be more intentional in what you are doing.

3. We recognize that there are some things in youth ministry that you can't control: the overall health and spiritual climate of the church, the family dynamics of the individual student, and so on. The "best practices" we'll be sharing with you are some things that you can control, or at least heavily influence. In other words, do what you can with what you've got.

We're fairly confident you won't agree with everything you read in these pages. But if you take the time to think and pray about how you can work these nine practices into your youth ministry context, we're equally confident the teenagers under your care will grow in their faith. And isn't that why we got into youth ministry in the first place?

We know books aren't cheap and your time is valuable. Thanks for investing a little bit of both.

Kurt and Tim

This is not a book about baseball. Because we aren't very good baseball players or big lovers of the game, it would be foolish for us to write a book about America's national pastime. Instead, this is a book about youth ministry. And because both of us are somewhat decent youth workers and big lovers of the "game," we thought it would be fun to write a book together about something that takes up so much of our time. Youth ministry is not America's national pastime, but we think it should be! And while we aren't qualified to write an entire book about baseball, we do know enough about it to paint a picture that we think will be helpful as you read these pages and contemplate prayerfully what the implications might be.

Baseball is a game played best with nine players. Sandlots and schoolyards are filled daily with patched-together teams of six or seven players, but baseball is a game played best when you can field nine—nine players, working together, each with a unique role. Fielding six or seven players is still baseball but not baseball at its fullest; it leaves some poor guy manning the entire outfield by himself thinking, "This is fun, but I sure wish we had all nine players!"

We'd like you to think of youth ministry in the same way. While you can certainly do good youth ministry and have fun doing it with only six or seven (or maybe even none) of these nine practices in place, you're missing out on the full experience. The EYM study shows that implementing all nine best practices—each with a unique role but working together—gives you the best chance for success.[1] We would hate for youth ministry to leave you out in left field. [2]

Most people who know a lot about baseball will tell you that all nine positions are important, but one seems to have the most influence on the game: the pitcher. Games are won or lost on the pitcher's mound, and without good pitching, not much else really matters.

Because my (Kurt) undergraduate degree was in religion, I decided not to go to seminary. Instead, after several years in full-time youth ministry, I went to graduate school to study leadership at Vanguard University.[3] The schedule of my program was such that we took four, one-week classes each year. We would spend all day, every day for an entire week taking one class; a few months later, we would reconvene for the next class. I'll never forget the frustration I felt when I looked at the class schedule and saw that our first topic was "The Soul of a Leader." I couldn't believe it! I was paying thousands of dollars to pursue my graduate degree in leadership, and the first thing we were studying was some nonsense about my soul?

---

1. Remember, we are defining success the same way the EYM study does: developing maturing Christian teenagers who are less likely to walk away from the church upon graduation.

2. This is not a book about baseball.

3. www.vanguard.edu

I quickly rushed across campus to my adviser's office to express my concerns. After hearing me out, my adviser, with a gentle grin on his face, simply said, "Kurt, I think you will really benefit from this class. In fact, I'm pretty certain it's exactly the class you need to take first." While I completely disagreed, I really didn't have much of a say in the matter; the course schedule was set and I would start my graduate studies in leadership by spending an entire week learning the importance of caring for my soul. To make a long story medium length, it turned out to be the best class of my entire grad school experience and, frankly, one of the best weeks of my life! We spent five days praying, journaling, reading, sharing the stories of our spiritual journeys, and examining our souls. (As you may have already figured out, mine was a bit dark and prideful!)

I (Tim) know of some youth ministries in my community that aren't as cool, well-funded, well-staffed, or large as mine. But if I were honest, some of these seem healthier than mine. In fact, they seem to have something mine doesn't. If I were really honest, I'd tell you that part of me is a little hacked off about their healthier vibe. But that would be shallow and unspiritual, so I won't be *that* honest.

We believe there's something missing from much of the discussion about youth ministry. Out of all the conversations, books, and articles we're hearing and reading, we believe there's something else, something less tangible and measurable, that we're not discussing: the spiritual vitality of the leader. If the leadership of the ministry isn't spiritually healthy, the ministry isn't spiritually healthy.

Can we say that again? *If the leadership of the ministry isn't spiritually healthy, the ministry isn't spiritually healthy.*

We are not proposing that our pursuit of God should be driven by our desire for healthy youth ministry. We are suggesting that the kind of growth and health and change we want to see in our students can only be brought by God's Holy Spirit, and an attempt to manufacture this growth by any other means will not work. Sure, by using our bag of tricks, we can provide most of the youth ministry "stuff" for our teenagers: lessons, retreats, camps, missions, music, and so on. But we can't conjure up true spiritual life change without God. We are at a severe deficit if we try to lead others to spiritual places we are not experiencing ourselves. It's awfully difficult to nurture someone else's soul if your own soul is neglected.

Just so you know, we're not claiming to have mastered this practice in our own lives. We need encouragement and accountability just like everyone else. We are all on a unique spiritual journey as our stories and God's story intersect, and we understand that we experience God in unique ways that fit our styles, spiritual giftedness, and personalities. Regardless of the specific spiritual disciplines you practice, there are some "big picture" principles that may help you nurture your own soul.

Before we look at those principles, it's important to recognize that the enemy of our soul would like nothing more than to see us ruined.

Be self-controlled and alert. Your enemy the devil prowls around like a roaring lion looking for someone to devour (1 Peter 5:8 NIV).

Most of you are mature enough in your faith to have passed the "getting devoured by the lion" stage of your spiritual journey. However, it is probably safe to say that all of us are susceptible to being slowly chewed apart. While there are certainly other tactics, we have identified several things Satan seems to use in his slow, steady attack of the soul. We call these the *Seven Soul Killers*.

1. **Discontentment:** Comparing, always wanting more of what you have, deciding that what you have isn't really what you want, believing the lie that the grass is always greener on the other side of the fence, and so on.[4]

2. **Busyness:** Overwork, living in a state of frenzy, anxiousness, not taking a day off, and similar patterns.

3. **Pride:** The Bible has a LOT to say about pride, and none of it is good!

4. **Selfishness:** The first line of Rick Warren's classic, *The Purpose Driven® Life*, says it well: "It's not about you!"[5]

5. **Entitlement:** When you begin to believe that you "deserve" certain things (such as a certain pay grade or a certain level of respect), you begin to kill your soul.

---

4. A friend of ours used to say, "The grass that's 'always greener' was fertilized by something."

5. Rick Warren, *The Purpose Driven Life* (Zondervan, 2002), 17.

6. Insecurity: Insecurity leads to a lack of confidence, comparing yourself to others, tearing others down to make yourself look better, constantly trying to win the approval of others, and a host of other ugly stuff.

7. Unresolved sin: While this sounds like a "catch all" category, the truth of the matter is that nothing will eat away at your soul like sin that you have chosen to ignore.

So, how does one combat these and other soul killers? We have some thoughts. Fair warning: None of these thoughts will be new or revolutionary to you, and you may be tempted to think to yourself, "Come on, guys, tell me something I don't know." We may not tell you something you don't know, but we'll tell you something we do know. We know that a shockingly high percentage of youth workers somehow have allowed the busyness of life and ministry to cause them to neglect some of the most basic and important practices.

Read the Bible well.

A while back, I (Tim) was interviewing for a youth ministry position at a great church. During the interview, someone from the search team asked me what I was currently reading in the Bible for my personal devotional life. I proudly shared a few deeply spiritual comments about my readings in the Gospel according to St. Luke and moved on. Later, someone from the search team asked about my current teaching topic with my youth group. I proudly shared a few deeply spiritual comments about my teaching from the Gospel according to St. Luke and moved on.

Confused, someone from the search team asked me what I was currently reading in the Bible for my *personal* devotional life. Confused, I proudly shared a few deeply spiritual comments about my readings in the Gospel according to St. Luke and moved on.

Do you see the disconnect? Do you ever struggle with the same thing? You probably spend quite a bit of time in God's Word, but how much of that time is spent for your own spiritual nurturing? Obviously God can use your lesson prep time to speak into your heart, but you must make sure you are setting time aside to allow God direct access to your own soul.

Jeff and Dawn Piekarski have the gift of hospitality (they prefer to call it the gift of "party"), and when they throw a party, people show up. Lots of people. It's not uncommon to show up at the Pies' (their affectionate nickname) house and find a crowd of current and former co-workers, clients, neighbors, acquaintances, and people they met in line at Wal-Mart. It's not the food that gets people to the Pies' house (though they are great cooks); Jeff and Dawn have the gift of making people feel welcome. They'll invite you in, and at some point during the evening one of them will end up seated across from you in their den or on their back deck asking you about your life and telling you about theirs. Sure, they are interested in learning some of the facts of your story, but they don't stop there. They truly enjoy getting to know people and forming friendships that last a lifetime. They want to know your story.

We believe our time reading God's Word should be similar. In the same way we spend time swapping stories with our friends so we can get to know them better, we should learn to read the Scriptures as God's story—not only to learn facts, but also to get to know the Storyteller more deeply. For me (Tim), reading the Bible this way required a pretty significant change in my approach. I've been around some people who view the Bible as a book full of rules for living, and these people focus on the do's and don'ts and struggle getting to the relationship side of things. I've been around other people who view the Bible as something they're obligated to read, and they read it begrudgingly in order to check off a box. But I've been around some who view the Bible as a book that gives life, and they read the Bible to nurture their soul. The difference may be subtle, but I wonder if our desire to read the Bible would increase if we read the Bible better.

Pray out of a genuine desire to connect with God.

We would make the case that prayer may be the best gift God has given his children.[6] The ability to enter into conversation with our heavenly Father, the creator of the universe, anytime we want is an opportunity granted to all Christ-followers. Prayer is a time for us to open ourselves up to God in an act of intimacy, a way for God to change our perspective, and an opportunity to connect more deeply with God. Grab hold of the picture Eugene Peterson paints of prayer.

Don't fret or worry. Instead of worrying, pray. Let petitions and praises shape your worries into prayers, letting God know your concerns. Before you know it, a sense of God's wholeness, everything coming together for good, will come and settle you down.

---

6. We're not slighting Jesus here. We recognize and believe that Jesus is our high priest making intercession on our behalf (Hebrews 4:14ff). We're just really excited that through prayer, we have the gift of ongoing communication with God.

It's wonderful what happens when Christ displaces worry at the center of your life (Philippians 4:6-7 The Message).

I (Tim) really like praying, but I usually feel like I do it poorly. Similar to reading the Bible, I was taught to pray out of necessity. I remember learning the ACTS (adoration, confession, thanksgiving, supplication) "method" of prayer as a young adult, and I've wondered often how God feels about our praying according to a method.[7] When I read John 17 (which I consider Jesus' most revealing prayer) and try to methodize it, I struggle. In John 17, Jesus is praying out a desire to be more deeply connected with his Abba. Jesus prays with passion and intensity, not with a list or a notebook. I'm not criticizing lists or journals—I use them both. I'm only suggesting that prayer is bigger than any prayer formula or list of requests.

Imagine how frustrated my wife would be if I started my conversation with her by consulting a list of things I wanted to talk about, then abruptly ended when I covered the last item.[8] Not only is my wife more relationally complex and interdependent than a list, she's from Texas; that exchange wouldn't end well. (Is it too obvious to make a "strikeout" joke here?)[9]

---

7. I'm not being critical of the ACTS method—I still use it at times as a prayer guide. I am suggesting that we must teach the parallel truth that prayer is an act of relational intimacy more than a formula.

8. In case you didn't recognize it, I was being sarcastic. I know, it wasn't good sarcasm, but it was sarcasm, nonetheless.

9. This is not a book about baseball.

Now imagine if I started the conversation by telling her how lovely she was, how much I appreciated the things she had done that day for me and our family, how lucky I was that she's my wife, and asking her to give input on the things in my life. And imagine, after all that, if I asked her how her day was going.

Some of you might be thinking, "That's great marital advice, but I thought we were talking about prayer." I hear you, and part of me agrees with you, but doesn't God paint the picture of the church being the bride of Christ? Don't we have entire books of the Bible that use the husband-wife relationship to reflect our relationship with God personally and corporately? Talking about prayer this way may sound a bit corny, but it might help you open up to your Creator in a way that is fresh and vibrant, and it might help God speak love, grace, and truth into your life in a way that is new and alive and much needed.

Life is full of worries and stress, and when you add youth ministry to the mix, it can get goofy in a hurry. Prayer is the best defense against the relentless attack of worry and stress on your soul. Entering into prayer because you want to—not because you are supposed to as a youth worker—might allow you to stay in the game a few more innings.[10]

Trust God in your own life.

Heath was a bully when I (Tim) was in seventh grade. He was a lot smaller than I was, but I was scared of him. I remember one of Heath's favorite games was taking something that belonged to me, holding it over a mud puddle (or a trash container or a lit match), and taunting me

---

10. This is not a book about baseball.

repeatedly, "Do you trust me? Do you trust me?" as he decided whether or not to destroy the item of the day. I never knew whether to tell him the truth and say, "No, I don't trust you, and I hope you lose all control of your bowels," or lie to him and say, "Yes, I trust you, and I hope you lose all control of your bowels." Heath was completely untrustworthy. That's not totally true; I could completely trust him to ruin my stuff! I'm so thankful that God, who is committed to helping me live life to the fullest, is not like Heath, who seemed fully committed to messing with me as often as possible.

Trusting God is a no-brainer, right? God loves us, wants what's best for us, always has our best interests at heart, and is completely trustworthy. But do we really trust God in good times as well as when the chips are down?

Trusting God means believing the truths of Scripture so much that we're willing to follow those principles, no matter how much (or little) sense they make. It means making wise choices about things like personal purity, trusting that when God says to guard my heart and my eyes, he knows what he's talking about.[11] Trusting God means choosing not to "get away" with things, even though no one would catch me or even though I think I deserve it. It means making the tough decisions that I know are right, even though I'll never get applause for making them.

---

11. A brief endnote doesn't do the topic justice, but we feel compelled to scratch the surface in this section. We're not trained to counsel the deeper issues related to pornography and addiction, but we've seen firsthand how devastating the effects can be. If you're struggling, please, please, please seek out help. Among many others, www.xxxchurch.com provides anonymous help for Christ-followers who are struggling with pornography addiction. Use their website as a launching pad to find more resources to help your walk to wholeness and wellness.

Trusting God means living with integrity in my personal life, my work habits, my business practices, and all other areas of life. Trusting God nurtures my soul because it allows the creator of the universe to take responsibility for the things I'm not big enough to manage on my own.

Find some ministry mentors.

When I (Kurt) think of the ways God has blessed me, something always finds its way toward the top of my list: God always has provided mentors to coach and encourage me along the way. When Rachel and I were newlyweds serving in our first church, God provided us with Rick and Melisa Williams, a volunteer couple who were just a little older and further along in their faith. In our next church, God provided us with Pat and Cissi Hickerson, an amazing couple who had children in our ministry. Upon our arrival at Saddleback, we met Don and Karolyn Thompson, who took us under their wings. These couples had a few things in common: They were a little bit older and wiser than us, they loved us unconditionally, they wanted the best for us, and they weren't afraid to speak truthfully into our lives. I am convinced that a major reason Rachel and I have survived in youth ministry for so long is because of the role these amazing men and women have played in our lives.

There is certainly a place for an accountability partner or two, but deep accountability doesn't always need to be part of a mentoring relationship. We are making the case for the importance of surrounding yourself with people who can pour into your life and nurture your spiritual, personal, relational, and ministerial growth.

The people who have filled this role in my life are such a gift. I cherish their friendships and thank God for them regularly. I don't deserve the love they show, but I receive it gladly. I can't encourage you enough to seek out men and women who will show you the same level of love and concern.

Practice the Sabbath.

Upon completion of the marvelous work of creation, God rested. I (Kurt) have often wondered why God needed to rest. Perhaps God rested to show us that rest is an honorable endeavor—it doesn't mean a person who rests is lazy or unmotivated. Maybe God rested because he wanted to set an example for us, knowing that an eventually sin-filled world would thrust humanity into a whirlwind of activity, and we would need to find rest and peace. The kind of peace originally offered in the Garden of Eden would become vital to the well-being of our souls. That's the scenario I've always envisioned and the one I still find most realistic. Of course, it's possible that since God wasn't getting interrupted with e-mails and wasting time online downloading funny videos, he actually finished a major project earlier than he expected. I don't know why God rested; I just know he did.

Marva Dawn wrote a great book exploring the Sabbath, where she comments, "A great benefit of Sabbath keeping is that we learn to let God take care of us—not by becoming passive and lazy, but in the freedom of giving up our feeble attempts to be God in our own lives."[12]

---

12. Marva Dawn, *Keeping the Sabbath Wholly* (Eerdmans, 1989), 4.

The rhythms you develop to experience God's care may be fluid, but choosing not to make rest a priority is choosing to take yourself out of the game.[13] Neither Tim nor I have this completely figured out, but we are working on it and have discovered a few ways to help our efforts.

1. **Protect your day off.** You probably don't get more than one full day off a week, and no one is as concerned about it as you are, so protect it.

2. **Take "seasonal sabbaticals."** Few of us will ever experience the freedom to take a prolonged chunk of time off to refresh our souls through a sabbatical. But you may have the ability to take one full day each season to rest, relax, and refresh your soul.

3. **Create a "time-out" strategy.** This simply means scheduling rest into your routine. A time-out strategy could look something like this: one hour a day, one day a week, one extra day per season, one week per year.

4. **Learn to say no.** This skill is not easy, but it is one of the most important a youth worker can learn. There are times when you can't say no, so take advantage of the times you can.

5. **Slow down, even when you're busy.** My (Kurt) boss, Rick Warren, likes to talk about the "slow down principle," and uses a good word-picture to make his point. Imagine taking a trip

---

13. This is not a book about baseball.

from coast to coast in an airplane. You would travel at 500 mph at an altitude of 30,000 feet. You would get there quickly, but think of all the scenery you would miss. Now take the same trip on a train; take the same trip in a car; take the same trip on foot! The point: Walking across the country is ludicrous. No, that's not the point. The point is that the slower you allow yourself to move, the more you see, hear, and smell. The slower you allow yourself to move, the more memories you make, the more people you encounter, and the less frazzled you feel. The nature of church work makes it hard to slow down, so look for opportunities to practice the art.

Maximize the positive influences.

We once heard Bill Hybels say, "There are two types of people in the world, those who drain you and those who charge you." The idea is that since you will never be completely free from being around people who drain you (we are talking about youth ministry, after all), you need to spend plenty of time around people who charge you up! Spend time with your spouse, with your family, with other people you love, with people who make you laugh, with people who encourage you, and with people who energize your life and charge you up. Doing so will give you more ability to go extra innings[14] with people who drain you without your tank becoming completely empty.

---

14. This is not a book about baseball.

Find your identity in who you are, not what you do.

Youth ministry is likely to creep into every aspect of your life if left unchecked. When this happens, we may begin to discover that we are finding our identity in our role as a youth worker instead of as a handcrafted child of God. We saved this one for last because, quite frankly, it is this identity confusion that leads so many youth workers into patterns of behavior that slowly but surely erode the soul. The warning signs are too many to count, but let's count to five just for fun:

1. Doing whatever it takes to be viewed as "cool" by our students.

2. Making sure youth workers from other churches know how big our youth group is.

3. Being more concerned with being funny than being biblically sound when teaching.

4. Positioning for influence and recognition by church leadership.

5. Thinking to yourself, "Why do average guys like Kurt and Tim get to write books, while brilliant thinkers like myself don't?"

It isn't easy to live confidently with the mindset that says, "I'm one of God's kids. God knew what he was doing when he created me. And living for an audience of One is all that matters." We all need to be reminded of this powerful truth from time to time. So let us remind you: You are one of God's kids. God did know what he was doing when he created you. And living for an audience of One really is all that matters.

Nurturing your own soul is as important to youth ministry as a pitcher is to baseball.[15]

For personal reflection:

1. How well do you feel like you are implementing this practice?

    _____ weak

    _____ average

    _____ strong

2. Is there a "soul nurturing" practice/discipline that jumped out from the rest?

3. Which of the *Seven Soul Killers* resonates with you the most?

4. Do you struggle with "identity confusion"? What is a pattern of behavior that points this out?

---

15. Though this seems repetitive, this is not a book about baseball.

Experiential option:

Write a prayer to God that expresses your feelings and learnings from this chapter. Keep it someplace handy, so you can refer to it when you feel you are in need of some quick "soul care."

BEST PRACTICE

BUILD AN AWARENESS OF GOD'S ACTIVE PRESENCE

EYM Marker for a Mature Faith:
*The ministry has a sense of the presence
and activity of a living God*

I (Tim) remember my first "God moment." I was a teenager, very young in my faith, at SuperSummer—my first church summer camp. It was Thursday, the last night of camp, and the speaker shared a powerful and emotional message. Tears were streaming down my face as I began to sense God's love in a deep way. That night, in that moment, I experienced God in a real way. Most of us are good at seeing God in the big moments, the "bells and whistles" times when something big—good or bad—happens and God shows up in a real and tangible way. But what about life's everyday moments? How do we recognize God's presence during the ordinary times? Here's a tougher question: How do we help teenagers begin to build an awareness of the presence of God in every aspect of their lives? See if you recognize these conversations in your own ministries.

Julie sat down on the couch in my office with a look of angst on her face. She's a 16-year-old high school junior and usually a bit melodramatic, but today she looked tired and frustrated and confused. "I just can't decide whether or not I should break up with Brian. I know he's not a good influence on me. Some of the things he wants me to do aren't right. And sometimes he says mean things to me. All my friends and my parents are telling me to be done with him. I know you don't think he's a good influence. And even in my quiet time this morning, I think God might have been telling me I should break up with him. What should I do?" I remember thinking, "How can you not know what to do? God is speaking to you through every person in your life—including yourself!" I also remember thinking, "Tim, how is it that Julie, a girl who has spent most of her high school years attending your youth group, doesn't sense that God is at work in her life?"

Douglas was fiddling with the glove compartment and not saying much. He's a 17-year-old high school senior, a natural leader, and a new Christ-follower, excited about sharing his faith. When I asked him what was wrong, he said he had been praying for the right time to tell his best buddy about Jesus but was getting frustrated that the timing never seemed right. He said, "All he talks about is how much he and his parents fight, or how he feels lonely a lot, or how he doesn't know what he wants to do with his life. There's just never a good time to tell him about Jesus." I remember thinking, "Dude, God is giving tons of open doors; you've just got to recognize them and walk through them!" I also remember thinking, "Tim, what are you doing to help kids like Douglas recognize the promptings of God and his Spirit?"

Let's review a little math. Remember the transitivity property of an equivalence relation? (We didn't either, but Google did.) The transitive property says if A=B and B=C then A=C. If that's true, and if we believe God is a supernatural, spiritual being, and if we believe God is alive and present in all of life, a logical conclusion is to believe that all of life is spiritual. We want students to live life not *hoping* for God to interact with them throughout their day, but *expecting* God to interact with them, because God loves them and likes them and wants to be with them. Simply put, we want teenagers to live with the understanding that Jesus made his home among us 2,000 years ago, he makes his home with us today, and they can view all of life through this simple but wonderfully profound spiritual lens.

One night during our youth ministry service, I (Tim) decided to have an "open forum" moment and asked teenagers to talk for a moment about what God had done in their lives the previous week. The question was confusing to them, and their silence was a little embarrassing to me. (I wasn't embarrassed of them; I was embarrassed that I had not realized I was doing these students a disservice by not building into our programming a habit and a system of talking regularly about God's activity in our lives.) If they realized God had been at work in their lives that week, they certainly didn't know they were allowed to talk about it! From that night on, I set out to help them understand that God was present in every aspect of their lives, and that the ability to recognize God's work and presence was an important and exciting part of their relationship with him.

How different might things be if all Christ-followers viewed every aspect of life as spiritual and if we all lived with a purposeful acknowledgment of God's active presence? I believe we would treat others differently, we would react to situations differently, and we would experience virtually every aspect of life differently. So where do we start? We start by helping teenagers embrace an accurate picture of the nature of God. If they view God like Darth Vader—tough, heartless, stiff, and with a deep, raspy voice—they may be afraid of his presence, afraid of the "Help! I can't breathe!" death grip. If they view God like Yoda—frail, wrinkly, wispy hair, and a comical voice—scoff at his relevance to life, they might. If they view God like Princess Leia—moody, cool clothes, funky hair—they may…well, who knows how they'd respond, but it couldn't be good! The point is, we have to provide plenty of teaching and learning opportunities around the topic of "Who is God?" to help teenagers learn to love God and begin to recognize the ways he works in their lives.

Our ministries can help students begin to recognize God's presence by tweaking some of the things we are already doing. In our worship gatherings and prayer times, we can regularly inject Scripture readings that express the reality of God's presence in our lives.

So the Word became human and made his home among us. He was full of unfailing love and faithfulness. And we have seen his glory, the glory of the Father's one and only Son (John 1:14 NLT).

We can teach on the incarnation of Jesus as the ultimate expression of God's presence among us and the Holy Spirit as God's continued activity in our lives. We can help teenagers recognize the ways God intervenes on our behalf. We can coach them to "pray without ceasing" and teach them to "practice" God's presence in our everyday lives.[16]

Several years ago, for our 10th wedding anniversary, I (Kurt) took my wife to Hawaii. Because I am a junior high worker, making junior high worker wages, we had never been before and have never been back! And because we knew it was a once-in-a-lifetime experience, we began "prepping" for the trip way in advance. We read up on all things Hawaii, we talked to people who had been there, we saved like crazy, we listed the things we wanted to do while we were there, and we talked constantly about our expectations for the trip. Despite the hole I put in my face while surfing, the trip was everything we hoped it would be, and more. Hawaii delivered big time! I'm certain that part of the reason Hawaii delivered such a wonderful experience was because of what we brought to the table. We expected it to be amazing, we planned for it to be amazing, and we sacrificed financially to help make it amazing. We did our part, and Hawaii did its part.

Imagine if we brought these same attitudes—preparation, sacrifice, and expectancy—to our daily walk with Jesus. I believe God would deliver— big time! Building an awareness of God's active presence is almost impossible if teenagers don't *expect* God to be involved in their everyday lives.

---

16. Brother Lawrence. *Practicing the Presence of God* (Paraclete Press, 2007). Thanks, Brother Lawrence.

We need to help them understand that they should bring some things "to the table" and that there will certainly be a few "hole in the face" moments in their journey, but when they expect God to be present, he will deliver—big time!

Here are a few suggestions that might help your students begin to create an awareness of God's active presence.

Use "God Talk."

Teenagers must come to believe God is at work in the world around them in order to understand the spiritual side of life. Once they begin to see God's action in the stories of the Bible, they gain the capacity to recognize more readily God's action in their own lives. The story of Moses and Miriam is a great example that reveals lots of truths about God's interaction with humanity. (Because the majority of the stories in the Bible are about men, make sure you're highlighting stories about the women God moved through as well.) With a quick concordance search, we can find numerous passages and stories that help to shape our understanding of God's benevolent work on our behalf. Do word studies on phrases that communicate God's activity: "God created," "God asked," "God said." Various forms of the phrase "God said" appear nearly 2,500 times in the NIV; God is active in the lives of his followers!

Remember the "open forum" story I (Tim) shared earlier? As embarrassing as that was at the time, the outflow of that experience was my commitment to do a better job of training teenagers to look for God's action in their everyday lives and be able to share it with their friends. Our youth group in Baton Rouge took this training seriously, and something pretty unique happened in our midst. I wouldn't call it a revival, but the conversations these students began having with their peers began to stir a minor awakening that changed lives and built connections that are still vibrant today.

Teach students to actively look for God's action in their lives, and celebrate times when they recognize it. Create space in your gatherings for people to talk about what God is doing in their lives. Give them opportunities to share what God is saying to them. Reclaim phrases like the one used by early Christ-followers in Acts 15:28, *"It seemed good to the Holy Spirit and to us…"* (NIV). Redeem biblical words like "blessed," and remind students that the undeserved love God shows to us is a gift. Make God the subject of sentences about our lives. Let God be the primary actor in our lives and our conversations as we strive to shape teenagers and be shaped by the Holy Spirit to be more like Jesus.

My (Kurt) wife and I are in the middle of the journey of raising two teenagers, Kayla and Cole. Not too long ago Rachel made a comment that stung a little bit, but I couldn't deny its accuracy. "It seems like as a family we talk a lot about youth group, church, our mission trips, and all the things we do, but we rarely talk about all the great stuff God is doing in our daily lives. We need to make sure Kayla and Cole don't just see God at work in the organized church, but that they see him at work in every aspect of their lives." As usual, Rachel was right in her observation. (She will read this book and insist the percentage is higher, but I'm going to put her at a 97 percent rating of getting things right; about the only time she is wrong is when she points out flaws in me.) Since that time, we have made a conscious effort to use more personal "God talk" with Kayla and Cole around the dinner table, while driving in the car, while hanging out at the skate park, and in other settings.

A fantastic and fairly simple tweak to your ministry setting may be merely to look for ways in your current programming to get teenagers talking more freely and more often about God's work in their lives.

Craft worship experiences that highlight God's active nature.

Most youth groups that meet regularly for youth worship have some sort of liturgy. It may not be a high church, formal schedule, but we have an order of service (and ironically, "liturgy" means "service") that we follow pretty consistently. Leonard Sweet's EPIC acrostic—Experientially, Participatory, Image-driven, Connected[17]—is a good reminder of how today's adolescents process information and could be a useful liturgy "creativity check." Regardless of the height of your group's liturgy, consider sprinkling in some additional elements that may help your teenagers practice focusing on God's active presence in their lives. You don't have to change your entire lineup, just adjust the batting order a bit.[18] Here are a few ideas:

> **1. Expectation.** Include a "call to worship" that is a passage, reading, or prayer that expresses an understanding that God desires to meet with his followers and an expectation that God will be present. You could also ask teenagers simply to

---

17. Leonard Sweet, *Post-Modern Pilgrims* (B&H Books, 2000).

18. This is not a book about baseball.

share their expectation for the worship gathering—what do they hope/want/need to get out of it?

2. Reverence. This balance is difficult to strike, but we must find a way to hold in tension the truth of the personal, approachable nature of God (Abba) with the corporate, holy nature of God (Alpha and Omega). Include readings about God as King on his throne and readings about the compassion of this King.

3. Connection/Engagement. God is both personal and communal. By design, corporate worship gatherings are communal. Plan times during your gatherings for students to connect their week with God's story. Invite them to give brief updates on what God is doing in their lives.

4. Response. When we are confronted with truth, we must make a choice. Include a decision time in your worship gatherings. It may not be appropriate to have an altar call each time, but give students an opportunity to respond and yield themselves to God. And let teenagers who make decisions share their stories with the rest of the group.

I (Tim) am glad to see the increased appreciation for various forms of worship that challenge the traditional thinking that "worship" equals music only. In our setting, we have incorporated painting, sculpting, dancing, writing, and other creative expressions as ways to engage students in a worship experience. All of these are great worship expressions, but sometimes I wonder if in our desire to make worship more than music, we have neglected music as a vibrant part of a worship experience. There are tons of great songs that speak to the activity and presence of God. One way to maximize music in your ministry is to purposely include a fair number of songs that reinforce the truth that God is active and present in the lives of his children.

One of the most significant transitions we (still Tim) made in our worship planning was moving away from compartmentalizing various aspects of a gathering—prayer, music, teaching, and video, for example—and beginning to plan in movements. We began asking, "What journey do we want to take students on?" and began charting a course to take them there. Functionally, the order may not look much different than before, but as we began thinking in "chunks" of a gathering, our creativity soared as we optimized our starting lineup.[19] And the intentionality we brought to the table allowed us to highlight God's active presence in the lives of students.

Make prayer a pursuit of God's presence.

Too often, prayer becomes little more than giving God a list of things we want him to do for us. Since we believe the Bible, we believe that asking God for things is part of a healthy prayer life. (See Matthew 7:7-11, Luke 11:5-8, and similar passages.) But it's only part of a healthy prayer life.

---

19. This is not a book about baseball.

Prayer is ultimately about communing with God. It's about our being aware of and practicing God's presence. It's two-way communication where we bare our souls to God, share our thoughts, feelings, hurts, and desires, and invite God to speak into our lives. Healthy prayer is less about our "to do" lists for God and more about God shaping our perspectives as we walk through life with him. Prayer is inviting God to be active in our lives. To some extent, the more we pray, the more we are saying that we trust and need God. Conversely, the less we pray, the more we are saying that we don't trust or need God. In fact, we might be able to say prayer is less about us and more about God.

Can we ask a really difficult question? When and how often do you pray with your students? We're assuming you teach about prayer, but how well do you model it? And when you do pray with them, do you model a "to do" list prayer or an "I trust you" prayer? It's a subtle difference but an important one. Here are a few examples of "I trust you" prayers:

- "Father, you are good all the time…and we know you always want the best for us…"

- "Lord, I don't understand why these difficult things are happening [could be personal struggles or global catastrophes], but I trust you, no matter what …"

- "God, the Bible says you know the number of hairs on our head and that you notice when a sparrow falls to the ground. Because of this, we trust that you are fully aware of our life journeys…"

The Bible is a gift that allows us to understand God and ourselves more clearly. Prayer is a gift that allows us to connect with God deeply and intimately. We need to teach and model prayer in this way to help our young people learn to recognize God's voice and to be aware of God's active presence in their lives.

Recapture the language of calling.

For several years, I (Tim) helped plant a church in suburban Baltimore. For good and bad reasons, we were described as (accused of?) being emergent, emerging, Bible-light, liberal, fundamental, watered down, and on and on. You name it, we were called it. We made lots of mistakes, but one thing we did well was value the importance of everyone in our community living on mission. Not just the clergy, paid staff, or volunteer leaders, but everyone.

We've noticed that in recent years, in a legitimate effort to emphasize that all Christ-followers have significance in the kingdom of God, the view of clergy or "professional ministers" has been downplayed. We fully agree with the need to diminish the artificial separation between the professionals and the laity, but we believe the solution isn't to hold a lower view of the professionals, but a higher view of the laity.

...You have been chosen by God himself—you are priests of the King, you are holy and pure, you are God's very own—all this so that you may show to others how God called you out of the darkness into his wonderful light (1 Peter 2:9 TLB).

The Bible has numerous stories of God calling people into his kingdom purposes. God calls some people for a lifetime of service. God calls some people for specific purposes. God calls some people for specific tasks. God calls some people for specific seasons. The bottom line: God calls all Christ-followers—not just vocational ministers or specially gifted individuals, but everyone—to get in the game.[20] When students grasp this truth and how it should shape their identity as Christ-followers, they can better understand how and why God is an active presence in their lives.

While still humbled and honored by God's calling, those of us who have embraced a life of vocational ministry may find it easier to embrace this truth than new Christ-followers or those with a particularly high degree of respect for the "professionals." Like most Christ-followers, adolescents also struggle with this concept. In fact, teenagers may struggle with it more because far too many churches send messages that reinforce the idea that God only uses older, more mature believers. Our favorite: "Teenagers are the church of tomorrow" (just writing that makes us roll our eyes in disgust).

Don't let anyone look down on you for being young. Instead, make your speech, behavior, love, faith, and purity an example for other believers (1 Timothy 4:12 GW).

Of course, teenagers aren't the future of the church; they are the church of today!

---

20. This is not a book about baseball.

Tell personal stories of your own awareness of God's presence.

Everyone loves stories. Some of the best songwriters are those who tell their tales in two verses, a bridge, and a chorus. The novelists we appreciate most are those whose books weave their yarns in a way that makes the reader get lost in the story. Those of you who are still reading this chapter (thanks, by the way) probably were distracted at some moments (when Kurt was writing) and refocused in others (when Tim told a humorous anecdote). Everyone loves stories.

As a leader in your youth ministry, you should tell your stories to your students. As you teach, preach, lead, and learn together, nothing communicates the truths of God like your personal stories. Isn't that what we tell our teenagers about sharing their faith? "The only authority on your story is you," and, "No one can argue with your story." The same applies as we build an awareness of God's presence in the lives of our students. Tell them how God pursued you to become a follower of Christ. Tell them how you knew God was calling you into ministry. Tell the story of how you knew you'd met "the one" you'd marry—or how you're trusting God on the journey of finding "the one." Tell a story of how you heard God speaking to you last week! Tell a failure story of a time you sensed God's direction and failed to follow his lead (Kurt wanted to include that last one because those seem to be the only stories he has). Students want to learn how to hear God; tell them your stories.

If you're a "paid, professional youth worker," ask other youth workers to share their stories as well. Bubby Boudreaux (yes, that really is his name) was one of the most effective youth workers I (Tim) have ever served with. He wasn't super eloquent, biblically trained, or even tactful. But he had a genuine love for Jesus that came out in his normal conversations. Students loved Bubby, and they wanted to hang out with him because the only agenda he brought to the table was to help people know Jesus like he did. One of his favorite methods was telling stories, and he had some zingers! You may not have a Bubby in your group (if you do, please let me know), but you probably have a few adult volunteers who are good at telling stories of their relationships with God. Look for them, and ask them to become storytellers.

Early in this book is probably a good time to remind you that none of these nine "best practices" are silver bullets that individually or corporately will guarantee that every student under your care will grow in their faith and continue to walk with Jesus after their youth ministry days are over. But we all want to give them the best chance at this, don't we? Certainly we want to help stack the odds in their favor. It makes sense that teenagers who understand God's active, present nature and live a life that experiences it would be more likely to maintain a vibrant, ongoing relationship with their heavenly Father.

For personal reflection:

1. How well do you feel like you are implementing this practice?

   _____ weak

   _____ average

   _____ strong

2. What "small tweaks" might you make to your youth ministry gatherings that will help students develop an awareness of God's active presence?

3. How much "God talk" is there in your youth ministry? How can you foster an environment where it becomes more common?

4. Can you identify students in your ministry who have experienced God's active presence firsthand and may be willing to share their story?

Experiential option:

Take 30 minutes and create list of "God Moments" from your life. What was happening in your life each time? How did God's presence show up?

BEST PRACTICE 3

ENCOURAGE PERSONAL SPIRITUAL GROWTH

EYM Marker for a Mature Faith:
The ministry emphasizes spiritual growth, discipleship, and vocation

The following may be one of the most painful scenarios in youth ministry. It's also one of the most common: A student who was highly involved in your ministry, served on a ministry team, invited friends to church, welcomed your presence and input into their lives, and genuinely seemed to "get it," graduates from high school and simultaneously "graduates" from their faith.[21]

Sound familiar? It does to us, too. Why does this happen? Why do students step off the field onto the bench?[22] According to the EYM study, a major contributor to this epidemic is simply (and by "simply" we mean simply defined, not so simply rectified) this: These students have not learned the value and importance of personal spiritual growth. Chances are they've heard of the idea, but they haven't moved from "knowing" about spiritual growth to "owning" spiritual growth.

---

21. We don't know who coined the phrase "graduate from their faith," but Doug Fields says it quite a bit so we are going to credit him with it. Of course it may not have been him, but it certainly wasn't us! If you said it first, e-mail us at timandkurtrippedmeoff@gmail.com.

22. This is not a book about baseball.

Most youth workers believe helping students grow spiritually is a key component of their ministries. Few of those same youth workers have defined what "growing spiritually" actually means or what it looks like. Still fewer are evaluating honestly whether or not they are accomplishing what they've identified as a key component of their ministries. The good news is, if you've never thought about what "growing spiritually" looks like for a teenager, you're not alone; the bad news is, we all have lots of work to do! We strongly encourage you to spend some time in the very near future landing on a definition and picture of spiritual growth that you aim for as you lead your ministry. But for now, let's use ours.

Spiritual growth is a lifelong process of loving God more and loving people more. (It seems like Jesus concurs; see Matthew 22:37-40.) Spiritual growth is supported and driven by healthy spiritual rhythms or practices (which we'll unpack in this chapter). Spiritual growth is evidenced by Christ-followers who are living and revealing the kingdom of God[23] in their families, schools, neighborhoods, jobs, teams, clubs, and other areas of life. In short, spiritual growth is a lifelong journey with Jesus, learning to trust him more every day as we spend time with him and other Christ-followers as we carry the gospel into all of our relationships by our actions and with our words.[24]

---

23. "Live and reveal the kingdom of God" (LaRK) is the mission statement from the church I (Tim) was a part of in suburban Baltimore, Maryland. We describe LaRKing as choosing to live the way of Jesus everyday in all things, big and small, and intentionally revealing the gospel in our actions and words. Sometimes churches focus on one or the other; we believe both are equally important. (See the next footnote.)

24. We'll unpack this missional concept more later, but a great website that helps us flesh out what missional means is www.friendofmissional.org. We want to say clearly that we believe missional living involves living AND revealing the kingdom of God, actions AND words, mercy AND evangelism. One without the other is an incomplete gospel. More on this in chapter four.

We've noticed that most youth workers who have landed on a definition of "growing spiritually" and have gone extra innings[25] by actually implementing some sort of strategy or method or structure or program to help it happen almost always fall into one of two camps. Either they create strategies or methods or structures or programs that their ministry provides for students to attend, or they create strategies or methods or structures or programs almost completely void of ministerial or adult input at all, leaving spiritual growth solely up to the individual student. The former develops young people who rely on their youth ministry to provide their spiritual growth, which typically works until the student graduates and is no longer involved in the ongoing efforts of the youth ministry; at this point, the student lacks the skills to provide any means of spiritual growth on their own. The latter assumes that the majority of students are capable of developing spiritual habits and disciplines on their own, void of ministry and adult support, which typically works until—well, frankly, this approach hasn't proven to work very well at all. Although it sounds noble to help make students completely responsible for their own spiritual growth, there are at least two problems with the idea:

1. Most students aren't willing or able to figure out and incorporate spiritual disciplines into their lives on their own.

2. We could be wrong, but isn't this something youth ministry is supposed to help out with, anyway?

---

25. This is not a book about baseball.

We propose a both/and approach to help students grow spiritually, providing strategies/methods/structures/programs that rely on both the youth ministry structure and individual responsibility. A both/and approach does the hard work of equipping students to nurture their own soul while encouraging the significance of healthy Christian community. A both/and approach provides opportunities for teenagers to begin living and revealing the kingdom of God under the guidance of the youth ministry and nudges them toward a desire to do so on their own.

Think of it like the process of adolescent development. Healthy teenagers move from total childhood dependence on their parents to a healthy expression of interdependence; unhealthy teenagers continue to rely too heavily on their parents and never learn to function as an adult, or these teenagers move past interdependence to alienation from their parents. Likewise, healthy Christ-followers move from total dependence on spiritual parents for spiritual nourishment to a healthy interdependence of growing in community; unhealthy Christ-followers continue to rely too heavily on their spiritual parents and never learn to nurture their own spiritual health, or they become alienated from Christian community with the absence of their primary spiritual parent. Wow, that was a mouthful. Read it again; it makes sense. (If it doesn't make sense, blame Tim; he wrote that part.)

Over the years, we have occasionally heard people connected to our ministries ask for "deeper teaching" or "more meat," often referencing Hebrews 5:12 with an air of spiritual superiority. Sometimes it's students who think youth group is too shallow, and sometimes it's parents who think their child is the next C.S. Lewis. Either way, it's easy to see the irony of their request when you read Hebrews 5:12 in context with the surrounding verses:

We have much to say about this, but it is hard to explain because you are slow to learn. In fact, though by this time you ought to be teachers, you need someone to teach you the elementary truths of God's word all over again. You need milk, not solid food! Anyone who lives on milk, being still an infant, is not acquainted with the teaching about righteousness. But solid food is for the mature, who by constant use have trained themselves to distinguish good from evil (Hebrews 5:11-14 NIV).

Do you notice the argument from the writer of Hebrews? "You are slow to learn," and, "You ought to be teachers." These aren't complimentary statements, affirming those who are asking for meatier teaching. The word "slow" used here means "dull" or "slothful" in understanding! The writer is indicting the readers for not having "trained themselves." We're not writing this to attack those in our ministries who have asked for deeper teaching; we're highlighting the writer's argument that spiritually mature people are individuals who have *trained themselves* so they can become teachers.

How are we living this principle in our youth ministries? How are we training students to train themselves? What are we doing to move maturing students into teaching/leading roles? How can we encourage students to grow spiritually and translate their spiritual growth into living and revealing the kingdom of God? Here are a few ideas we like:

Emphasize that it's a personal choice to be a follower of Jesus.

I (Tim) am married to a beautiful, brilliant, and compassionate Christ-follower named Tasha. We met, fell in love, and got married in less than 11 months. We have an amazing marriage, and I'm proud to tell you that I am 50 percent committed to my wife! Not impressed? OK, I am 90 percent committed to my wife. Still not impressed? How about 99 percent committed? Come on, that's almost an A+!

Total, 100 percent commitment is the only thing that will make a marriage work, because a relationship is either committed or it's not. If I tell you I am 99 percent committed to my wife, you will immediately wonder about the 1 percent: "What's he holding back?" "What is he doing in that 1 percent of the time?" "What will his Texan wife do to him when she finds out?" We all know that a marriage with anything less than a 100 percent commitment is doomed, so we counsel engaged couples to wait until they're 100 percent sure. I wonder if we settle for less in the way we communicate with our students about a relationship with Jesus?

Jesus often *discouraged* his listeners from following him unless they were ready to commit completely. In Luke 14:25-33, Jesus gives the crowd multiple examples of reasons they shouldn't follow him unless they had counted the cost and were willing to go the distance. As youth workers, we must teach teenagers the same thing.

One hundred percent of youth ministries in the U.S. have some students who are only involved because they are forced by their parents to attend.[26] While not ideal, we think this is OK for a couple reasons. First, it helps

---

26. OK, we don't have statistical evidence of this, but we know it's true. Besides, 70 percent of statistics quoted in books are wrong.

your attendance numbers. (What youth ministry book would be complete without at least one "numbers" joke?) Second, it's OK because even reluctant students are being exposed to the One who loves them and, we hope, being challenged to make a personal decision to become a follower of Jesus—to develop a faith of their own instead of one mom and dad are forcing upon them.[27]

We need to teach students that following Jesus is the interplay of deeper knowledge, greater understanding, and personal choice. Obedience is a choice all Christ-followers must make on a daily basis. Obedience leads to more obedience as God proves himself to be trustworthy and loving. Obedience also leads to joy, peace, and purpose, as we yield more and more of our lives to Jesus. On the flip side, disobedience is also a choice we can make daily. Disobedience leads to more disobedience, as we become convinced that the way of Jesus doesn't work—even though we're not even giving it a chance! Disobedience leads to pain, sorrow, disappointment, and regret as we experience the truth of Paul's words in Galatians:

Don't be misled—you cannot mock the justice of God. You will always harvest what you plant (Galatians 6:7 NLT).

---

27. You may have noticed that we prefer the language of "following Jesus" over other phrases, because it connects a faith decision to action. After some good conversations with biblical scholars who are way smarter than us, we also prefer the word "trust" over the word "faith." It seems faith often is understood in incomplete ways, something closer to intellectual assent. On the other hand, trust is something that starts small and grows over time as the person I'm trusting demonstrates evidence of trustworthiness. But we're not Bible scholars, so you can ignore this endnote altogether.

One way to help students understand the short-term and long-term consequences of their decisions and how bad decisions lead to other bad decisions is a little game we call "Write Out the Ending." In this game, we ask students to think of something they're wrestling with (or to make it less intrusive, think of something an average teenager struggles with): alcohol or drug use, sexual activity, and so on. Then we ask students to spend some time thinking about and writing out what the likely ending to their story will be. We're amazed at how honest teenagers are in this little game, and you've just taught them the valuable skill of critical thinking and making good, wise choices.

Teach and model spiritual disciplines/practices/rhythms.

In most Christian traditions, personal and corporate spiritual disciplines are encouraged. You can find lots of good resources on teaching these to students. Here are a few of our ideas:

Help your students learn to read the Bible. Though it is at the core of our faith practice, few students (and to be honest, few adults) grasp the whole story of the Scriptures and how passages and books interrelate. The Bible is long, wordy, and complex, and sometimes it doesn't make a lot of sense. Encourage students to read whole books of the Bible at a time as a way to grab the overarching story. In the same way they read a novel—sometimes reading carefully, sometimes reading quickly—give them permission to read the Bible not to study, but to begin connecting the dots. Here are a few very simple ways to help students read God's Word in a more narrative way:

- Point them toward devotional books written just for teenagers.
- Encourage them to journal as they spend time in the Scriptures.
- Introduce them to some basic commentaries, Bible dictionaries, and other resources that will give them valuable insight into what they are reading.

Help your students learn to study the Bible. If we believe what the writer of Hebrews says, every word in Scripture is important and should be studied.

For the word of God is alive and powerful. It is sharper than the sharpest two-edged sword, cutting between soul and spirit, between joint and marrow. It exposes our innermost thoughts and desires (Hebrews 4:12 NLT).

We should teach students how to do inductive Bible study so they can study the Bible on their own or with a group of their peers—without depending on an adult to teach them. This approach teaches students to read the Bible as a cohesive unit, made up of smaller cohesive units. We want students to read the Bible in proper context, and traditional inductive Bible study methods include asking questions like, "Who is writing?" "To whom is the author writing?" and "What's going on in the world of the reader?" We also want students to ask questions like, "What does this passage teach me about God?" "What does this passage teach me about myself?" and "What does it teach me about how God loves people and how I should love people?" We should also provide our students with resources and teach them how to use a Bible handbook, a theological dictionary, and a commentary. If you don't feel comfortable with these things, bring in a designated hitter;[28] invite your pastor or someone trained to offer instruction to your students.[29]

Help your students learn to memorize the Bible. When I (Tim) was in high school, my youth worker led us through an intensive, 26-week study on spiritual disciplines. I wasn't too excited about lessons on memorizing Scripture…until my parents divorced, and I experienced a deep loneliness in my soul. Throughout this time in my life, God kept reminding of a verse I had to memorize for the study:

…God has said, "Never will I leave you; never will I forsake you"
(Hebrews 13:5 NIV).

God's Word is powerful stuff! Helping students develop a desire to read, study, and memorize it is a powerful and important part of helping them grow spiritually. Albert Einstein once said that he didn't memorize anything he could look up. Let's face it: The idea of memorizing Scripture doesn't sound exciting to most teenagers, and in our era of having everything at our fingertips, it's tempting to allow Scripture memorization to become a lost art. King David said that he hid God's Word in his heart to protect him from sin; that seems like a timeless idea! Here are a few ways to help your students memorize Scripture:

---

28. This is not a book about baseball.

29. A fantastic book that will help older students learn a few ways to study the bible is Rick Warren's *Bible Study Methods* (Zondervan, 2006).

- Curriculum usually provides a "key verse" for the week, but most youth workers don't do much with it! Challenge students to memorize the key verse from each week's lesson.
- In our (Kurt) ministry, we picked about 20 key verses and put them on key rings. We gave them away to any student who wanted them.
- Send a weekly text message with a memory verse. Buy a soda for every student who memorizes the verse.

Some youth workers have done away with the idea of encouraging Scripture memorization because they fear that students will focus on the act of memorization and miss the importance of implementation (be "doers" of the word, not just "hearers"). Let's be careful not to throw the baby out with the bathwater.

Teach and model a healthy prayer life for your students. Prayer is about reorienting our lives to what really matters. Many students have replaced the effort and time it takes to invest in a relationship with God with sports, academics, friends, work, and other commitments. Through prayer, we "re-place" our relationship with God in the center of our lives.

Don't worry about anything; instead, pray about everything; tell God your needs, and don't forget to thank him for his answers. If you do this, you will experience God's peace, which is far more wonderful than the human mind can understand. His peace will keep your thoughts and your hearts quiet and at rest as you trust in Christ Jesus (Philippians 4:6-7 TLB).

Several years ago I (Kurt) noticed that the vast majority of students who regularly attended my junior high ministry had a very childlike and almost lazy view of prayer. When pressed, most of them admitted that, at best, they rarely prayed for more than a minute or two as they were falling asleep, and at worst they actually used prayer as a method to *help* them fall asleep! I decided something had to be done. I hastily threw together a new program called R.A.P. (Rise And Pray) that would gather students together every Friday morning at 6 a.m. to pray for one hour before school. I never thought about the details of my idea, such as how junior high students would get to the church by 6 a.m. every Friday (I ended up driving from house to house to pick kids up) or the consequences of my idea—such as the fact that I now had to wake up at 5 a.m. every Friday. But it worked! For over a year, a couple dozen seventh- and eighth-graders met together once a week to pray. Years later, when I run into former members of that junior high group who are now adults, the conversation often turns to those days involved with R.A.P. More often than I like to admit, the stories revolve around students falling asleep in the corner and the numerous times they caught me asleep in the corner! But the stories always return to the fact that R.A.P. taught them the value of prayer and began in their lives the habit of seeking God that they still carry today.

Here's a simple idea that will help elevate prayer in your ministry: Instead of just saying, "I will pray for you," when a student shares a hurt, a need, or a concern, say it—and then do it right there! Pausing for a moment in the moment to pray with a teenager shows them that prayer is something of value.

Encourage students to find a friend or two who will "have their back" spiritually. We will be the first to admit that developing friendships that offer true accountability is tough. Most students won't take you up on your challenge to invite another like-minded friend access to the good, bad, and ugly parts of their lives. But for those who do, these types of friendships will prove to be an amazing (and challenging, and frustrating, and faith-stretching) piece of their spiritual growth. If we believe in the power and importance of relationships (which we do, and we will talk about in chapter six) then it makes sense that we believe a major part of the power of relationships is found in their ability to sharpen and strengthen us in our journey of faith.

While it's certainly possible for students to figure out how to sharpen and strengthen each other on their own, it's probably not likely. Every team needs good coaching.[30] Help your students learn to ask tough questions and give honest answers. Remind them that we aren't supposed to try to navigate life and faith all alone; we need each other!

As iron sharpens iron, so people can improve each other
(Proverbs 27:17 NCV).

A person standing alone can be attacked and defeated, but two can stand back-to-back and conquer. Three are even better, for a triple-braided cord is not easily broken (Ecclesiastes 4:12 NLT).

---

30. This is not a book about baseball.

Here are a few questions we encourage our students to ask one another:

1. How have you loved and pursued God this week?

2. How have you turned away from God? What sins are you struggling with, and how are you addressing them?

3. How have you seen God work in your life this week?

4. How have you loved others this week? Your mother and father and siblings? Your teachers, coaches, and bosses? Classmates, neighbors, co-workers?

5. How have you revealed the kingdom of God this week?

6. Is there anything you see in my life that may be hurting my relationship with Jesus?

We think helping students develop a list of accountability questions is a good idea because if your students are anything like ours, without some help their questions will look more like this:

1. What's your Gamerscore on Xbox Live?

2. Do you think we'll get in trouble if we ditch fifth period tomorrow?

3. How do I convince my parents to give me unlimited texting on my phone?

4. So, what did she say when you asked her out?

5. Have you heard the one about _____?

6. Um…Oh yeah, you don't hate God, do you?

Good questions, to be sure—just not all that helpful for spiritual growth.

Encourage adult volunteers to "get beneath the surface." Wisdom often comes with age, and teenagers desperately need Christ-following adults who are a little further down life's road to be involved in their lives. Challenge your adult volunteers to be on the lookout for opportunities to take their conversations with teenagers a little deeper. Encourage your students to open up and share their struggles, their questions, their doubts, their fears, their failures, their successes, their hopes, and their dreams with the adults in your ministry.

Because it's not always an easy thing to do, I (Kurt) give my adult leaders a few tips to help them in their efforts to get beneath the surface. For those of you who know me, it will come as no shock that each tip starts with the same letter.

> **1. Be Confident:** You love Jesus and you like teenagers. You have wisdom and insight to share. Be confident that God has placed you in the life of this student for a reason.

> **2. Be Consistent:** Begin to make these types of conversations a regular part of your relationships with students. We want our students to expect this type of relationship with you.

3. Be Compassionate: Be quick to listen and slow to speak. Reserve judgment for the stuff that really matters, and always let your love and compassion be what students see most in you.

Help students experience the joy of generosity. Regardless of your understanding of the tithe, it's tough to argue with Scripture's exhortation that everything we have is from God, and we are to be generous stewards of it. Not only does God expect us to give a portion back to him, he wants his followers to be responsible and generous with the rest of it as well! Helping students learn the basics of debt management, saving for the future, and other important topics will lay a foundation of financial responsibility that will free them up to experience the blessings that seem to follow those who give freely and generously. In our consumer-driven culture, it may be more important than ever to help our young people understand the relationship between financial stewardship and spiritual growth. And who knows—maybe students will lead their families to be better stewards of their resources.

Paint a bigger picture of God's kingdom. In our Introduction (what, you didn't read the intro!?!) we wrote—and want to make clear again—that we do not believe youth ministry is broken. We don't think the current way most churches are doing youth ministry is solely to blame for the rate at which students seem to leave church after high school. Putting all the blame on the current state of youth ministry makes for great back alley conversations at youth ministry conferences but isn't completely fair. (Thank you for listening; we will now step down from our "state of youth ministry" soapbox.)

But the current (and recent-past) youth ministry model has some characteristics that are worth reconsidering. Specifically, the way we have narrowed the kingdom awareness of our teenagers.

Far too many students who are active in their youth groups have a very limited picture of the body of Christ and the kingdom of God. Most youth groups have limited interaction with the rest of their local church family, rarely (if ever) partner with other youth groups in their area (especially youth groups of another denomination), and have little presence in the community. Yet these same groups pat themselves on the back because they do a service project or short-term mission trip once a year. Attendance at our programs seems to have become the ultimate goal.

Is it possible that for fear of losing a student's attendance at our youth group gatherings, we have withheld exposing them to and encouraging their involvement with other experiences within the body of Christ and his kingdom? When you grow their vision of the kingdom and their involvement in various aspects of it, you help them grow spiritually.

Help students discover and develop their spiritual gifts.

I (Tim) have a confession: I love tests—things like IQ tests, the Myers-Briggs Type Indicator, and Facebook™ quizzes (just kidding… sorta). I recognize I'm in the minority here, but I even like spiritual gift inventories. I've taken and given my share of stinkers, but for the most part, spiritual gift inventories are a great way to help your students understand their spiritual gifts. Isn't that Paul's main point in Ephesians

4:4-13? Take a few minutes and review this Ephesians passage. While you're at it, look over Romans 12:1-8 and 1 Corinthians 12–14. This stuff is a pretty big deal!

We're thrilled to know that leaders from various theological backgrounds are reading this book, and we have no interest in debating various understandings of spiritual gifts (or any other deep, theological topic). Go work out a healthy theology of spiritual gifts with folks in your context and teach it to your students. Whatever your theology may be, consider including a few discussions that will help frame a healthy understanding of gifts.

1. All spiritual gifts belong to the body of Christ for its building up, not to the person who is gifted in a certain way (Romans 12:5). The best way to combat selfishness with gifts is by solid teaching, not by guilt (though our grandmothers might disagree).

2. Passion and obedience must be balanced. Sometimes God calls us to serve in an area outside of our giftedness because the body of Christ needs a servant. Our passion for obedience should overshadow our passion to do what we like to do. (However, "doing what you like to do" is an important part of the experience, and we will look more deeply at this in chapter seven.)

3. Gifts come in seasons, and if we don't respect our gifts and use them as God desires, God may diminish the gift in our life (see Matthew 25:14-30).

Explain each spiritual gift in a way your students can understand them. Some students are sharp, and they'll understand the meaning of "exhortation" with minimal discussion. Other students are—well, less sharp?—and it takes them a little longer to understand things. Take whatever time you need to help students get a grasp of each spiritual gift. A great way to do this is by translating them into contemporary language. This doesn't have to be rocket science. For example: Exhortation is the "cheerleading" gift; hospitality is the "come over to my house" gift; and so on. You could even have your teenagers help you come up with new names for the gifts. (If they're good, let us know, would ya?)

Let students experiment with their spiritual gifts. Find opportunities for students with the gift of teaching to teach. After they teach, debrief with them to help them discover if the gift "inventory" lines up with their experience. Let the high school senior with the gift of hospitality host the seventh-grade lock-in at his parent's house. Of course this may only serve to uncover the fact that he has the gift of "throwing a kick-butt party" and his parents have the gift of "calling the po-po[31] on a bunch of seventh-graders." Try out the gift, debrief, and re-evaluate. And then try out the gift, debrief, and re-evaluate. Repeat as necessary, every year, over and over.

---

31. I (Tim) come from a long line of Southerners. As Jeff Foxworthy has revealed, Southerners like to shorten long words and phrases. In Louisiana and East Texas, the police are referred to as the "po-po." I don't know why.

Send students out to serve.

Among the complexities of student faith drift ("graduating" from faith after high school), serving others may be the most predictive issue that determines whether or not students stay connected to their faith. This is one criterion we must include when evaluating our ministries' success. If we're not preparing students to serve, we're not modeling the church of the New Testament. Some of you reading this chapter may disagree strongly. In most cases, we'd be OK with that. In this case, we'd like to try to convince you to change your mind.

In the Old Testament, God promised to bless Abraham and his descendants. Why? To be a blessing to all other nations.[32] In the Bible, we learn that God sent his Son into the world. We read that Jesus came to serve others, first the Jews, then the Gentiles. Throughout his ministry, Jesus sent out his disciples: as a group, in pairs, the 12 disciples, the 70 followers, and so on. At the end of Jesus' time on earth, before his ascension into heaven, he commissioned his followers to go into all the world, and he told them they would be his witnesses in Jerusalem, in Judea and Samaria, and to the ends of the earth.

We serve a sending God, and we must be a sending ministry. We believe true spiritual growth can be measured by the degree our students are living the "sent" life.[33]

---

32. Genesis 12:2

33. Jason Dukes, *Live Sent* (Wheatmark, 2009).

God is an incarnational God. In the same way God sent Jesus into the world, Jesus sends his followers into the world. In the same way that Jesus became human to go where humans live, Jesus sends out his followers to go where people are: neighborhoods, schools, workplaces, and so on. In the same way Jesus showed us how to live the kingdom of God, Jesus sends out his followers to be incarnations of the kingdom of God wherever they go. Healthy youth ministry must be incarnational as we send teenagers into places adults are not invited.

Something beautiful happens when students are incarnating Christ in their worlds. As teenagers act in faith, they begin to trust God more. Students depend more on God as they strive to reveal the kingdom of God. They lean on one another more as they realize they are aliens in a strange land. Alan Hirsch calls this experience *communitas*[34]—it means growing in their trust in God and their interdependence with one another. *Communitas* flows out of incarnational, missional living. *Communitas* happens when students serve inside and outside the body of Christ.

We like the idea of dividing service into two parts: Ministry is service inside the body of Christ, and missions is service outside the body of Christ. Ministry is about building up the body of Christ; missions is about adding people to the body of Christ.

Have you ever heard the old (and gross) saying, "Dead fish float downstream"? Let's not let this become a word-picture of our students'

---

34. Alan Hirsch, *The Forgotten Ways* (Brazos Press, 2007).

walk with Jesus. Building a youth ministry that helps teenagers grow spiritually—that walks beside them, holds their hand, equips, and empowers them to take the responsibility for their own growth—is no easy task. But it's a task worth undertaking. We need to do whatever it takes to get students off the bench and into the game.[35]

For personal reflection:

1. How well do you feel like you are implementing this practice?

_____ weak

_____ average

_____ strong

2. Can you think of a student or two in your ministry who seem ready to implement some of the spiritual disciplines we discussed? What might you do to encourage them to take this step?

3. In what ways might you paint a bigger picture of the kingdom of God for your students?

---

35. This is not a book about baseball.

4. Does your church encourage teenagers to use their gifts to serve and provide opportunities for them to do so? If not, what are some existing ministries within the church you might be able to convince to become "student friendly"?

Experiential option:

We want you to practice what we preach! Consider taking a fellow youth worker from your community out to lunch. Target somebody from a church that is vastly different from your own.

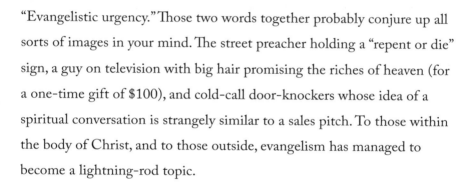

BEST PRACTICE 4

FOSTER A SENSE OF EVANGELISTIC URGENCY

EYM Marker for a Mature Faith:
The ministry promotes outreach and mission

"Evangelistic urgency." Those two words together probably conjure up all sorts of images in your mind. The street preacher holding a "repent or die" sign, a guy on television with big hair promising the riches of heaven (for a one-time gift of $100), and cold-call door-knockers whose idea of a spiritual conversation is strangely similar to a sales pitch. To those within the body of Christ, and to those outside, evangelism has managed to become a lightning-rod topic.

Because of this, we know this chapter will frustrate most of you on some level, at some point. Some of you will read this chapter and protest that we aren't pushing for more hell-focused altar calls (the "if you were to die tonight" contingent). Another segment of you will mutter under your breath that we're too fundamental and aren't arguing for more social action (the "give them food before you give them Jesus" contingent). Like most of you, we live in this tension daily. Please give us a little grace and fight the temptation to dismiss parts of this chapter because something we suggest doesn't line up with your theology, tradition, or methodology.

We're not trying to promote any one understanding of evangelism over another; we're simply trying to encourage you to keep evangelism—however your tradition expresses it—in your regular rotation.[36]

For the sake of clarity, let's state some assumptions that will influence the rest of this chapter: Evangelism means "sharing the gospel." The "gospel" is the "good news." The "good news" is the truth that the kingdom of God is made available to all through the redemptive work of Jesus Christ's life, death, and resurrection. Regardless of how you articulate the good news, fostering a sense of evangelistic urgency means building into students a clear understanding of the gospel and a driving, burning passion to share it with a broken world in need of some good news.

Recognizing that we all have nuanced understandings of the gospel based on our traditions and training, allow us to share some key elements that are common to the vast majority of us and are important to help students understand the good news:

1. **The gospel is about grace.** God loves us not because of our goodness, but in spite of our badness.

   But God demonstrates His own love toward us, in that while we were still sinners, Christ died for us (Romans 5:8 NKJV).

2. **The gospel is about forgiveness.** The sin of humanity separates us all from God, and only because of the sacrifice of Jesus can we be forgiven.

---

36. This is not a book about baseball.

The reward for sin is death, but the gift that God freely gives is everlasting life found in Christ Jesus our Lord (Romans 6:23 GW).

3. The gospel is about salvation. Through Jesus, God saves us from our past sins, our present despair, and our future destruction. God rewrites our destiny because of the life we can receive through Jesus.

That if you confess with your mouth, "Jesus is Lord," and believe in your heart that God raised him from the dead, you will be saved. For it is with your heart that you believe and are justified, and it is with your mouth that you confess and are saved (Romans 10:9-10 NIV).

4. The gospel is about hope. We live in a world broken by our own selfishness and rejection of God. The goodness of God overpowers the evil of Satan in the world, and we have hope for our todays and our tomorrows.

"Everyone who calls, 'Help, God!' gets help" (Romans 10:13 The Message).

5. The gospel is about mission. God saves us because he loves us, but our salvation is not all about us. Once we begin to follow Jesus, God wants to move through us to lead others to Jesus. God saves us to live and reveal his kingdom.

But how can they call on him to save them unless they believe in him? And how can they believe in him if they have never heard about him? And how can they hear about him unless someone tells them? And how will anyone go and tell them without being sent? That is why the Scriptures say, "How beautiful are the feet of messengers who bring good news!" (Romans 10:14-15 NLT).

Allow your tradition and training to shape your understanding of the good news, and whatever it is, teach it well to your students. And build in them an urgency to share the gospel with those God puts in their path. But here's the question: Because none of our students want to be associated with the negative images of evangelism we mentioned at the beginning of this chapter, how do we foster a sense of evangelistic urgency? How do we help them urgently want to participate in something most of them want nothing to do with?

Focus on the kingdom of God.

The kingdom of God is a big deal; it's life as God intends it to be lived. The kingdom of God can be well described with the word "shalom." Many of us know shalom to mean "peace," which is accurate. But shalom is so much more than peace. Shalom means wholeness, completion, rightness, and perfection.[37] Shalom is wholeness as God intended creation to experience in Eden—the kingdom of God.

But something happened to shalom in Eden. We broke it. We took the perfection of life as God intended it to be lived and decided we'd rather try Plan B. (And what a simply genius plan it was: "Eat this and you will become like God"—who wouldn't want that!)

---

37. W. E. Vine and Merrill F. Unger, *Vine's Complete Expository Dictionary of Old and New Testament Words* (Thomas Nelson, 1996).

The consequences of the sin in Eden were (and are) monstrous. Everything changed. Everything. God didn't abandon Adam and Eve, but things were no longer as God intended, and for all practical purposes, the picture of the kingdom of God was broken. Our relationship with God was broken, our relationships with one another were broken, and our relationship with the world around us was broken. And we still live in this reality today; things are not as they are supposed to be.

Jesus talked a lot about the kingdom of God. He said the kingdom of God is "at hand."[38] He said the kingdom of God is like a mustard seed and a bit of yeast and a farmer scattering seed.[39] Jesus lived a life that showed what the kingdom of God was all about: He lived in perfect oneness with the Father, with people, and with the created order. To Jesus, the kingdom was about more than heaven or hell, and he lived a life that brought God's desires for the world to the world. And Jesus called his followers to the same lifestyle, to be salt and light, to highlight the God flavors and colors of the world,[40] to show glimpses of what God intends for his creation, to be like yeast leavening bread and a farmer scattering seed. We are God's agents to help people experience restoration in their relationships with God, with people, and with the world around them. We are God's partners in restoring the kingdom of God and in helping God's will be done on earth as it is in heaven.

---

38. Matthew 3:2

39. Check out Matthew 13 for a cool list of these sayings.

40. Eugene Peterson's paraphrase of Matthew 5 in *The Message* is beautiful. Check it out.

The kingdom of God has been breaking into the world since Genesis, and it will continue to do so until Jesus returns and makes everything new. Jesus will one day restore perfectly what was lost in Eden; he'll make our broken, wounded, fractured world whole, complete, right, and perfect. Jesus will bring to completion our relationships with God, with people, and with the world around us.

One game I (Tim) like to play with students is "What If?" because it keeps us grounded in the "nothing is impossible" nature of God. Since the sin in Eden changed everything, and everything is broken, it's fun to envision what the world would be like if the kingdom of God was restored. Create space for students to ask, "What would [this] look like if it were restored?" I've asked that question while up front at our weekend youth worship gathering, and I've asked it in counseling sessions. I've asked it about students' relationships with their parents, and I've asked it about dating relationships. I've asked that question when bad things happened to good people, and when catastrophe struck whole countries. I've asked it while looking at the Colorado River, and I've asked it in the swamps in Louisiana. Playing the "What If?" game reminds our teenagers (and us) that the world we see today is still broken, still waiting, still "groaning and laboring" for Jesus' return. And until he returns, we are called to live and reveal the kingdom of God.

We've learned that when students begin to understand the kingdom of God, the gospel becomes more complete and they get more excited to let others in on it.

Help students understand and tell the story of God.

I (Tim) have some missionary friends serving in a very remote part of Africa, and since the Bible has not been translated into the native language of the people there, the missionaries "story" the Bible.[41] Starting in Genesis, the missionaries tell the major stories of the Scriptures, focusing on the central themes about God: strength, mercy, compassion, and so on. When the missionaries finally start telling the story of Jesus, the villagers immediately recognize that Jesus is God because he demonstrates the same strength, mercy, and compassion that they've learned about God. The villagers understand the big picture of the Bible, and that allows them to see how Jesus is a continuation (and culmination) of God's story.

Here's a simplified summary of the story of God as found in the Scriptures: God creates humans to be at one with him and one another; things are OK for a while, and eventually we choose poorly and get ourselves into a big mess that we can't fix; we repent, turn to God, and call out to him—sometimes through the Old Testament sacrificial system—and God hears us; God takes action on our behalf, forgives us, and restores our right relationship with him and one another; things are OK for a while, and eventually we choose poorly and get ourselves into a big mess; and on and on the story (cycle) goes. Rinse and repeat.

This story repeats itself in various ways throughout the Old Testament: the lives of individuals, the lives of families, the lives of tribes of people, the life of the nation of Israel. Eventually, the people begin to sense

---

41. If you're not familiar with storying the Bible, look it up. It's fascinating.

hope as the prophets and poets write of a coming Messiah who would break the cycle and bring restoration. In the New Testament, when Jesus finally arrives, the cycle is forever broken as Jesus makes a way for us to be right with God. Before Jesus ascends into heaven, he commissions his followers to continue to live and reveal the kingdom of God. As he announces that his departure is not permanent, Jesus reminds his followers—then and now—that the story is not over. For now, we're in the seventh-inning stretch, waiting for the game to be wrapped up so we can go home.[42] We live in the "in between" of God's story, and we've been commissioned to tell the story and invite others into it.

A great way to build the understanding of the story into the lives of your students is to give little reminders each time you teach. Whenever you teach, spend two minutes highlighting how the story of God fits into the lesson. When you teach from a specific book of the Bible, comment briefly how that books fits into the overall story of God. When you teach a topical lesson, connect it to God's story. I (Kurt) have a friend, Alan Mercer, who wraps every single lesson on every single topic into the story of God. For instance, when he is talking about friendships, he shares that part of the reason friendships struggle is because of the brokenness of the world we live in, which is because of sin—but redemption is possible through Christ. And this redemption should impact our friendships! (That's my short example; Alan would give a much more articulate example!) He believes strongly that if students have good understandings of God's story and see how it impacts every aspect of their lives, they are much more likely to live and reveal the kingdom.

---

42. This is not a book about baseball.

The story of God is evident in our culture in many ways: movies, music, television programs, books, news, commercials, and so on. We can tell the story of God simply by highlighting the glimpses we see. We can tell the story through singing (well, Kurt can't), acting, creating, preaching, teaching, and so on. We must tell the story, and we must equip our students to do the same.

Emphasize the reality of God's active presence.

We explored this point in detail in chapter two, but it's worth repeating here briefly to see how the nine practices are interconnected. As we help our students recognize God's active presence in their lives, they begin to connect God's story to the world's story. When they connect God's story to the world's story, they can see how those two stories connect to their own story. And understanding these three stories—God's story, the world's story, and their story—and an awareness of how they are all connected will give students a new sense of confidence to share these stories with their friends. Quick quiz: How many times is the word "connect" used in the above paragraph? We like that word.

Teach a respect of all people.

A member of his church once told a pastor friend of ours, "I feel comfortable inviting you to the same parties I attend with my un-churched friends because I know you won't make them feel uncomfortable; you'll make them feel valued." What a wonderful compliment! It sounds like something people would have said to Jesus back in his day. It's interesting that the "worst" people in society were the ones who felt most comfortable around Jesus; Jesus almost never offended sinners. It was the religious people who had issues with him, and the biggest issue they had was that he didn't seem to have any issues with sinners! How different might our world be if those of us who follow Jesus were willing to spend just a little bit more time in the company of those who don't yet know him.

It's unfortunate, but Christ-followers have reputations for being terrible listeners to people with differing viewpoints. I (Tim) remember a conversation between a pastor friend and a skeptic. The skeptic had not finished asking her question when the pastor interrupted and began answering the question she hadn't finished asking. When the skeptic tried to interject to clarify a point or ask another question, the pastor would talk louder until the skeptic eventually stopped talking altogether. At the end of the "conversation," the pastor felt pretty good about remembering the counter-arguments he learned in seminary, and I'm sure the skeptic's doubts were confirmed—Christ-followers are rude.

If we Christ-followers expect pre-believers[43] to listen to us, it's only fair that we listen to them—and not just pretend to listen while we organize our spiritual laws or Roman Road.[44] By definition, a spiritual conversation must have two-way communication. One-sided badgering does not qualify for "spiritual conversation" status.

---

43. Randy Millwood changed our thinking about those who are not yet Christ-followers by recognizing them as pre-believers. The simple semantics remind us that Jesus should fill us with hope that everyone might come to trust in him.

44. We are not making negative comments about either of these evangelism methods. We are suggesting that these methods are most effective in the context of a relationship between a Christ-follower and a pre-Christian.

Jonathan, a pastor friend of ours, told the story of baptizing a longtime atheist who finally chose to follow Jesus. The former atheist told Jonathan that a key factor in him remaining open to Jesus was Jonathan's treatment of him with respect and care, even though the atheist had rejected Jonathan's invitation to follow Jesus. I (Kurt) must confess, there have been some people that I've basically written off after I've shared the gospel with them. I told them that they could call me if they ever changed their mind, and I moved on. I didn't mean it that way, but my actions communicated that they were only significant if they believed like I did. We must help teenagers learn to respect and love people before, during, and after they share the good news.

Teach the importance of going where people are.

In our Introduction (what, you didn't read the intro?!?) we mentioned that we met at a camp in Alaska. As part of the trip, we were treated to an amazing day with a chartered tour guide who flew us in a tiny little pontoon plane to a little lake in the remote Alaskan wilderness. As we were exiting the plane, he mentioned the fact that bears would likely smell us cleaning the fish we caught and that he needed to grab his bear repellent. His "bear repellent" turned out to be a 12-gauge shotgun he held between his legs the entire time we fished. Kurt hasn't fished since, but I (Tim) love to fish. The whole experience is enjoyable for me: deciding where to go, researching the type of fish I'm after, buying the right lures and gear, prepping the boat, riding to the right spot, setting up, catching the fish, cleaning the fish, eating the fish (I don't practice catch and release; I practice deep fry and enjoy), and telling the tale. Though my favorite target is largemouth bass in the bayous of Louisiana, I've fished for lots of different fish in lots of different places. But one thing I've never done was catch fish in my living room. For some reason, all the prep work—talking about fishing, reading about fishing, setting up my gear—is useless if I don't go to a lake.

Some of you probably don't like the use of a fishing analogy, but we figure if a fishing analogy was good enough for Jesus, it's good enough for us! Here's the bottom line: We must do a better job of helping students understand the power of *going*. While it's important for students to bring their friends to our programs (in fact, we'll write about that in the next section of this chapter), we handicap their ability to share the gospel if they only *bring* and never *go*.

Here's where it gets simple: Your students probably don't have to go very far because they're already swimming in the same lake as their friends. They just need some encouragement to break free from their little school of Christian fish and go spend time with other fish once in a while. OK, that may be taking the fishing analogy too far. Sorry, Jesus.

Sometimes the act of "going" can be made easier when students recognize that God made each of us unique and wants to leverage our uniqueness to reach others who are similar to us. (Isn't that an oxymoron? "You're unique, just like everybody else!") Some of your students are athletes; help them recognize that God made them athletic to bring the gospel to other athletes. Some are musicians; help them recognize that God made them musical to bring the gospel to other musicians. This is true of every student in your ministry: skaters, technology geeks, mathletes (you know who you are), and so on. Jesus became human so he could come to where we lived, and he sends us into our circles of influences so we can bring Jesus to the people we're most like. This is incarnational ministry at its finest.

When I (Kurt) was a young, ambitious, and somewhat dumb youth worker, I was troubled by the fact that very few of the students in my youth group seemed equipped to share their faith or had any desire to do so. My fix: Ask them to memorize a canned gospel presentation and take them to the beach to approach (accost?) strangers with said presentation. The results were borderline horrific, not because nobody that goes to the beach is open to the gospel, but because most people who go to the beach, or anywhere else, aren't open to having their activities suddenly interrupted by somebody they don't know, wanting to talk about something they aren't interested in. Helping my students learn how to articulate the good news of Jesus and share it with others was a fantastic idea; asking 12-year-olds to try to share it with strangers at the beach wasn't.

Obviously we aren't suggesting that students should only care about and share the gospel with people they know and have stuff in common with, but we are suggesting that in a time when most Christ-followers have never shared their faith, it may not be a bad place to start.[45]

---

45. Like so many others, this statistic is hard to verify, but it is estimated that close to 75 percent of Christ-followers have never shared their faith with a pre-Christian. That's like seven batters in your starting lineup never getting a hit! But remember, this is not a book about baseball.

The Apostle Paul makes a great point that's worth exploring a bit.

Yes, whatever a person is like, I try to find common ground with him so that he will let me tell him about Christ and let Christ save him
(1 Corinthians 9:22 TLB).

We should teach our students the importance of finding common ground with people of a variety of backgrounds; this seems to be what Paul is saying. But notice in this passage that the crux of what he says is that he finds from his own background points of contact with people. Paul is not becoming someone he's not; he's connecting with people out of who he is. Helping teenagers identify and embrace their uniqueness (which is not always an easy task when working with adolescents) is a vital part of increasing their confidence to share their faith. They no longer have to play out of position[46] and try to "be like somebody else" but can share their story, God's story, and the world's story with a sense of confidence.

Allow us to make one final comment related to the urgency of "going." Sometimes, as we reach young people for Christ and begin discipling them, we unintentionally (and sometimes purposefully) begin to separate them from their circle of friends who are not Christ-followers. We appreciate the need for students to have healthy friends who help them make wise decisions, but how are we helping them become salt and light if we separate them from people God has yet to reach? We recognize the tension we're drawing, but we believe it's important to coach students in

---

46. This is not a book about baseball.

a way that they don't become so immersed in the Christian ghetto[47] that they're unable to relate to others who are not Christ-followers.

Challenge your students to invite their friends to be a part of your community.

In *The Celtic Way of Evangelism*, George Hunter III shared how Patrick's (a Christian missionary to the Celts) method of evangelism differed from the contemporary methods of his day. Hunter summarized the Roman process as presentation, decision, fellowship—people believed before they belonged. After studying the Irish culture, Patrick contextualized evangelism by reversing the Roman model. Patrick's strategy was fellowship (community), ministry and conversations, and belief/commitment. Where previous models presented the formula for reaching people as "get them to believe," then "help them to belong," Patrick found that for the Celts, they weren't going to believe until they felt they belonged. We think Patrick's method is fitting for today's teenagers.[48]

Your youth ministry should be a place where non-believing students can begin to feel like they belong to the community of believers. Because "belong" often comes before "belief," you can replace some of the pressure your students may feel to lead somebody to Christ with the challenge to invite them to hang out with your youth group events and/or programs. And once students feel like they belong with God's family, they may be more interested in being adopted *into* God's family.

---

47. The Christian ghetto is the isolated space many who call themselves Christ-followers inhabit. It has its own language, music, books, magazines, movies, and so on. Among others, Bob Briner addresses the Christian ghetto in his book Roaring Lambs.

48. George Hunter III, *The Celtic Way of Evangelism* (Abingdon Press, 2000).

So, how do we help unbelieving students feel like they belong? Here are a few ideas to get you started.

First, seeking students need to see that Christ-followers are not weirdos—we're just normal people with a greater sense of purpose, passion, love, and joy. Christ-followers get terrible press. Sadly, what most people know about us is what they read about in the headlines or see on the news. Images of famous pastors caught in a moral failure, abortion-clinic bombers, and hate groups hiding behind proof-texts are what keep so many from wanting anything to do with the God these people profess to love. They also need to have broken the perception of the boring, safe, sissy Christ-follower. When a student who is unfamiliar with Jesus shows up to your youth group and realizes that most of their perceptions and stereotypes of Christ-followers are wrong, that students who love Jesus are somewhat normal, they will feel much more comfortable.

Second, take the time to evaluate how your youth group "feels" to a student who is new to church. Do guests[49] feel welcomed? Are they greeted, shown around, and introduced to others, or are they left to fend for themselves? Are current youth group members excited to see them? How quickly are they judged for not knowing when to stand up and when to sit down, for not eagerly participating in the singing time, for sending a text message during the lesson, or for breaking any other of your youth group's many, many, many, many standards of appropriate behavior? Do your youth group's "feel" and "culture" assume that everybody has insider information about Jesus, church, and standards?

---

49. Can we make a plea to use the word "guest" instead of "visitor"? Not only does it feel more welcoming, it sounds nicer, too.

Third, err on the side of interested instead of disinterested. Seek out your first-time guests, ask them questions about themselves, and get to know them. After youth group is over, ask them if they enjoyed their time, if they have any questions about what they experienced, and other engaging questions. We have found this is much more effective if done by other students than when done by the adults. The junior high ministry at Willow Creek Community Church has a ministry they call SNAP (Showing New People Around—yes, they know the letters are out of order). The students involved in SNAP have made a commitment to seek out first-time guests and do everything possible to help them feel like they belong.

Fourth, go out of your way to let guests know that you're glad they joined you. Follow up through a handwritten note, a phone call, a Facebook™ post, a text message, or whatever form of communication is most effective with teenagers as you read these words. Again, this is much more effective when it's done by students. There are tons of ways to make sure guests feel welcomed and appreciated, and all of them are good—with the possible exception of a creepy 43-year-old male youth worker knocking on the door of a seventh-grade female who visited youth group the week before.

Encourage students to be "trust builders."

For many pre-Christian teenagers, their openness to the gospel hinges on whether or not they trust Christians.[50] A student who distrusts Christians, whether because of pre-conceived perceptions or because

---

50. Don Everts and Doug Schaupp, *I Once Was Lost: What Postmodern Skeptics Taught Us About Their Path to Jesus* (IVP Books, 2008).

of an experience based in reality, is rarely ready to hear an articulated presentation of the gospel. This allows us to replace the urgency of "I need to go out and tell everybody about Jesus" with "I need to go out and build trust with my friends who don't know Jesus so they will be open to what I have to say when the time comes." It's funny to me (Kurt) that many people will read this as a timid approach to evangelism. After all, teenagers are going to hell unless they hear the good news of Christ. True, but is it possible that to somebody who has a distrust of Christians, the "good news" doesn't sound so good? Maybe instead of challenging our students to get out there and talk about Jesus to anybody who will listen, we should challenge them to look for ways to break down the walls of distrust so many of their friends have concerning people who claim to have experienced the love of Christ.

If you ask me (and even if you don't) I would cast my vote that almost anybody can muster up the courage to approach a stranger and present the case for the need for Jesus. But far fewer people can do the hard work of seeking out relationships with those who don't know Jesus, building trust with them, and wisely looking for an opportunity to have a spiritual conversation. One of the best ways to build trust is to begin to bridge the gaps.

Bridge the gaps.

Along with other misunderstandings, some pre-Christians have the terrible misconception that Christ-followers are bigots. The way many perceive Christ-followers is often more about anger, judgment, and narrow-mindedness than love and mercy. We're not suggesting that

Christ-followers compromise their beliefs or ignore the hard truths of the Scriptures, but we are suggesting that we teach the whole counsel of the Bible to our students. In addition to Paul's letters to the church about lifestyle issues, we read Paul's words that say without love, we're noisy nothings with nothing to gain.[51]

Dr. Martin Luther King Jr. said that 11 a.m. on Sunday morning was the most segregated hour in America. Whether that statement is factually true or not, Dr. King's observation is still valid today. Part of living and revealing the kingdom of God and preaching a whole gospel is promoting reconciliation in our lives and communities. Teaching on these issues, partnering with diverse groups, and valuing in your words and actions the mutual benefits of relationships among diverse churches are all ways you can bridge gaps in your youth group.

Addressing and responding to issues such as race, culture, and language are easy, because they are God-created differences, not choices people are making. Our responses to those are clearly guided by the Scriptures, and these gaps can be fairly easily bridged by studying relevant passages from the Bible.

There is neither Jew nor Greek, slave nor free, male nor female, for you are all one in Christ Jesus (Galatians 3:28 NIV).

In his book *The Hole in our Gospel*, Richard Stears writes, "Being a Christian or follower of Jesus Christ requires much more than just having a personal and transforming relationship with God.

---

51. 1 Corinthians 13

It also entails a public and transforming relationship with the world."[52] As we build an evangelistic urgency in the lives of our students, we must teach and preach a whole gospel of personal reconciliation and a pursuit of justice.

Balance "urgency" with patience.

For years I (Kurt) owned a car that I didn't like but had been pressured into buying. The whole thing started when I walked into the Ford dealership to kill some time by browsing the used car area on my way home from our church gathering. My wife and I were in the market for a new car and had already agreed that buying from a dealership was NOT the best plan. As I hustled through the lot, I made a crucial mistake: I slowed down enough for an eager salesman to catch my attention. Within mere seconds of our introduction, he had me standing in front of a car that would meet our needs and fit our budget. The price seemed too good to be true, and when I mentioned this to the salesman he made sure to point out: "This price is only good today; if you come back tomorrow this deal will be off the table." I asked a few more questions and, after taking it for a test-drive, I decided it wasn't the car for me. The salesman, however, wasn't accepting my decision. "Look, I can take another $500 off the price. You won't find a car anywhere that is nearly as clean as this for anywhere close to the same price. But this price is only good today; if you come back tomorrow this deal will be off the table." After a few more rounds of "I don't think this is the car for us"/"This deal will be off the table tomorrow," I bought the car.

52. Richard Stearns, *The Hole in Our Gospel* (Thomas Nelson, 2009), 2.

I didn't really like that particular model, I didn't like the color, and I hadn't talked things through with Rachel. But a pushy salesman convinced me that I didn't want the deal to be taken off the table. The results: a car I didn't want (that I paid off in 60 easy payments; I tried to sell it but apparently nobody else wanted it either), a frustrated wife, and resentment for pushy car salesmen.

This scenario parallels how so many of youth ministry's evangelistic efforts often look. Because we have a heart for pre-Christian students, youth workers often become pushy salespeople who present the gospel in a way that makes it feel as if God's "deal" of grace and forgiveness might be off the table tomorrow. Thus, lines like "If you were to die tonight, do you know where you would spend eternity?" are used in an urgent attempt to get teenagers to buy into a relationship with Jesus. Here's what we have learned over the years:

1. The vast majority of students don't die tonight.

2. God's grace is never "off the table."

3. A pushy approach to evangelism often results in resentment that hurts the cause of Christ in the long term.

Students desperately need to hear the gospel. God's story is too important to neglect, and we can't naively hope that pre-Christian teenagers will stumble upon God's grace and forgiveness by themselves. Balancing this urgency with a sense of patience and trust in God's sovereignty is not an easy task. But it's one worth pursuing.

Today's students sense and experience the brokenness of the world, so equip them to share the gospel with anyone and everyone they meet as they live and reveal the kingdom of God.

For personal reflection:

1. How well do you feel like you are implementing this practice?

    _____ weak

    _____ average

    _____ strong

2. Think of some of your most "involved" students. How many of them do you think you are capable of communicating God's story to one of their friends?

3. What might you do to help your students begin to identify how God's story and the world's story connect to their own story?

4. Can you identify anything in your youth ministry setting that, instead of "bridging gaps," is actually widening them?

Experiential option:

We used the analogy of a fishing trip to talk about the importance of going where people are. Take some time to think of another analogy that may work better with your students, in your context.

INCREASE THE CONGREGATION'S APPRECIATION OF STUDENTS

EYM Marker for a Mature Faith:
*There is a congregational priority
and support for youth ministry*

In a small church I (Tim) served in Louisiana, our growing little youth group needed a new place to meet. In the church building was a decent-sized storage room that was full of junk, and I thought it would be cool to recover that space and turn it into a youth room. I got permission from the powers that be, borrowed a pickup truck, bought some paint, and invited people to meet me the following Saturday. It was awesome. The students and volunteers caught the vision, and we had a blast moving furniture and boxes, creatively painting the walls, and arranging the new room. It was awesome!

That day unified our group in a very cool way, and for the next three months that room was THE place for our students to hang out—and then something changed. The leadership of the church decided that every room in the church building, including our new youth room, needed to be "of uniform color." Without letting me speak into the decision or the potential consequences, they agreed that the new youth room needed to comply and quickly repainted it a lovely shade of white. Our students and volunteer leaders were crushed, and I was left in the position of trying to convince them that the decision wasn't an indication of how the church felt about our youth group. And honestly, I don't think it was. The youth room wasn't the only victim of the paint rollers of doom; as promised, every room in the church was painted "of uniform color." And while I know the church and its leaders valued our youth ministry, this decision communicated something different to our teenagers.

Sadly, you probably have your own examples. Your students come home from summer camp fired up about Jesus, and a deacon fumes at the group because the church van has Doritos crumbs on the floor. You get lots of spiritual momentum from a weekend retreat, and the first thing the pastor does when he sees you is complain about the Coke stains on the carpet in the foyer. (Who puts carpet in a foyer, anyway!?!) The first church I (Kurt) served at was a wonderful church that valued youth ministry; the fact that it was in the late '80s and they had a full-time junior high worker to minister to about 50 junior highers makes that clear. Like most growing churches, ours was constantly trying to figure out how to maximize our space to accommodate the crowd. During a pastoral staff meeting, we were trying to figure out what to do with our ever-growing elementary department, and I somehow managed to lose my junior high meeting space in a matter of about 45 seconds. The conversation went like this:

> Children's Pastor: "We are dying for more space. I think we should swap with the junior high ministry because their space is huge and all they do is run around and play games."

Kurt: "Um...we do more than just play games."

Sr. Pastor: "Great, if you do more than just play games then you don't need such a big space; just don't play games for a while. Great idea, children's pastor!"

Kurt: "Um..."

Sr. Pastor: "What's next on the agenda?"

I had always admired my pastor's ability to make a quick decision.

Stories like these will always exist. Leading a church is a challenging proposition, and God has entrusted this task to flawed men and women doing the best they can and making tons of mistakes along the way.

System theorists believe an individual cannot change unless the system in which he or she lives also changes.[53] If your congregation is not healthy and doesn't have an appreciation of students, your youth ministry will struggle. A healthy congregation builds assets into the lives of its students, and these assets shape the students' views of God, of the church, and of their place within the church. A healthy congregation communicates—implicitly and explicitly—to teenagers that they are loved, valued, appreciated, needed, and wanted. A healthy congregation lays a significant foundation for healthy, long-term ministry with youth.

An unhealthy congregation with a lack of appreciation for teenagers communicates to them that they are a nuisance, that they're in the way, and that they're not wanted.

---

53. Virginia Satir, in particular.

These words are rarely spoken to students, but they will get the message. An unhealthy congregation wounds students and plants in them seeds of cynicism and skepticism that will damage their capacity to connect with a church community later in life.

So are we saying that a church congregation that doesn't appreciate students is an unhealthy church? Yes. But we won't let churches off that easily because most churches will say they appreciate students. And while that may be true, many choose to show their "appreciation" from a distance. It could be likened to the wealthy, absentee father who says he loves his children (and probably does) and tries to prove his love through providing nice things rather than sharing life with his kids and spending quality time together. A truly healthy church doesn't merely provide great resources for student ministry and hope young people feel valued as a result. Instead, a healthy church looks for ways to share life and spend quality time with the students in the body. This is how we would define "appreciation" in this conversation.

Here are the stages of congregational appreciation we developed to help you identify where your church is and to give you something to shoot for. Based on our above definition, you will see that we believe most churches don't truly appreciate students. We also believe that you need to be very wise in how you choose to articulate this to your church because it won't be easy news to hear.

> **1. Informed:** At the very least, the church body needs to know you exist and what is happening. Believe it or not, a lot of

churches aren't even living in this stage. In many churches, the left hand truly has no idea what the right hand is doing most of the time.

2. **Interested:** When the church is well-informed, interest begins to rise. In this stage, the church body moves from a mindset of "Well, I guess we have to give them some space in the bulletin" to "We love to hear what God is doing in our youth ministry!" This is where a majority of churches live. It's not a bad place to be, because once the church is interested in what's happening in the lives of its teenagers, it becomes much easier to move forward.

3. **Involved:** In this stage, adults from the church body "switch silos" and begin to serve in the youth ministry. Occasionally, the youth ministry will look for ways to do the same. This has been the model for youth ministry for much of its history. Here, the church provides quality resources for student ministries and emphasizes the importance of adults being involved. The youth group and the rest of the church like each other, support each other, and value each other.

4. **Intertwined:** A formal youth ministry still exists, but it exists within, not separate from, the life of the church. In this stage, adult/teenager interaction moves from a proclaimed value that everyone agrees with but few participate in to a lifestyle of the church. Not many youth ministries are intertwined, because it takes significant intentional effort to get here and stay here.

We believe that true appreciation of students begins in stage three and comes to fruition in stage four. While you're not able to exert total control over moving your church through the progression, you do play a significant role. In the next few pages, we'd like to share some practical ways you can increase your congregation's appreciation of teenagers. The first two suggestions may feel a bit out of place, but they serve to lay a foundation upon which you can begin to build.

Be a team player.

We're shocked at the attitude of numerous youth workers we've met who feel that they should get a proverbial "blank check" from the congregation to do whatever they want, whenever they want, however they want, at whatever the cost. They want to be free to focus solely on students without any expectations to contribute in other areas. If this were a book about baseball, we would say that lots of youth workers view themselves as the superstar on the team who should be allowed to show up late to spring training, skip team meetings, and be offered the best locker in the clubhouse.[54] You hurt your own cause when you allow yourself to be perceived as uninterested in and unwilling to be part of the bigger team picture. Here are three easy ways to practice being a team player:

> 1. Raise your hand in staff meeting and volunteer to head up a project that isn't youth ministry-related.

> 2. Find a ministry in your church with an upcoming big event and ask how you, your leaders, and your students can help out.

---

54. This is not a book about baseball.

3. Instead of always "fighting for more" (more budget, more help, more space), voluntarily sacrifice something so it can be allocated to another ministry.

The value of being a team player is one of the most valuable lessons I (Kurt) have learned in my youth ministry career. Caring only about youth ministry, protecting my time so I can focus only on students, and fighting hard to make sure we get what we need has often gained short-term results but has always hurt in the long run.

Be professional.

I (Tim) confess that for years I believed if I didn't dress cool, speak cool, act cool, and interact cool, students wouldn't respond (keep in mind that my "cool" is significantly less cool than lots of other people's "cool," but I was trying). To be honest, it might have worked a little. Some of the students seemed to respond to me and even sort of identified with me when I acted like a teenager. The problem was, just as the students viewed me as a wannabe teenager, so did their parents, our adult volunteers, and the leadership of the church. In their eyes, I acted like a batboy who wanted to play ball in the big leagues.[55]

Somewhere along the way, youth workers began to associate professionalism with staleness, non-creativity, and uncoolness. (I don't know if that's a word, but if it's not it makes sense that I would be the one to coin it.) As I've grown in ministry, I've come to understand professionalism as the way I carry myself and interact with others related to the ministry I'm leading.

---

55. This is not a book about baseball.

Some simple things you might consider:

1. **Look at yourself.** Be true to yourself, but don't underestimate the power of appearances and first impressions. If you're a surfer, dress like a surfer, but be a professionally acting surfer (see Kurt for more info). If you're a longhaired hippie-type, dress like a longhaired hippie-type, but be a professionally acting longhaired hippie-type (see Tim for more info—partly because Kurt's window of opportunity for having long hair closed a few decades ago, and partly because Tim has the best hair in youth ministry). Be yourself, but recognize that as a youth worker, you are representing your church in a field that is constantly struggling to gain respect, and you should carry yourself in a way that helps the cause.

2. **Look at your watch.** Lots of you are carrying an unfair label of "disorganized" because a few bonehead youth workers don't mind making everyone else in a meeting wait 20 minutes while they swing by Starbucks for their venti mocha latte with steamed soy milk and no whipped cream. Then they forget the folder they need for the meeting that they were 20 minutes late for. Then they give uninformed answers because the answers to the questions being asked by parents at the meeting are in the folder! And the answers that are given are hard to understand because the youth worker is busy slurping his venti mocha latte with steamed soy milk and no whipped cream!

My (Kurt) biggest pet peeve is the youth worker who shows up late to meetings holding a (venti-sized) coffee cup full of mocha latte with steamed soy milk and no whipped cream.

3. Look at your calendar. Plan ahead, schedule wisely, and try not to make commitments you can't keep. Youth ministry is spontaneous, but most churches aren't. An easy way to increase the perception of yourself and the ministry you lead is to manage the calendar wisely.

As a certified ADHD youth worker, I (Tim) appreciate how unnatural this feels for many of us. We get caught up in the moment, we're highly relational, we love spontaneity, and we get distracted. (Squirrel!)[56] If you're like me, get some help. Hire an assistant; find someone to volunteer in the office; ask a parent to help you manage details. We youth workers, at some point, must learn how to be professional in our setting, especially if we want the congregation to appreciate what we're doing.

Once you're viewed as a team player who acts somewhat professionally, things begin to change. People like what they see, outside observers notice that you're doing good work, and everyone learns that you're competent to continue doing it. Ultimately trust is built, and when the church trusts the youth ministry and those who lead it, good things happen.

---

56. From the Pixar movie *Up*.

Tell youth ministry stories to anyone who'll listen.

Nothing communicates like a good story, so become a storyteller! When something positive happens in youth ministry, jot down a few sentences so you can tell others about it. When you get an encouraging e-mail from a parent about the changes they've seen in their teenager, pass it along to others. When a student makes a commitment to follow Jesus or takes spiritual steps forward or commits to anything worth celebrating, let others know what's going on. When you tell stories about youth ministry, you're not bragging on yourself—you're bragging on God!

If your church has an elder board or executive team or steering committee, ask if you can drop in to their monthly meetings to give them a youth ministry update. If you can't physically make the meeting, ask them if you can write up a few paragraphs letting them know what's going on. If they just approved the purchase of a new video camera for your youth group, make them a "thank you" DVD!

Get a list of adult Sunday school classes or small groups and ask the leaders if you can pop in their meetings to share about the youth ministry. Do the same for any group that will let you join them. Make an even bigger impact by inviting students to go with you, and let them tell their own stories. You might also invite adult groups to pop in on the youth ministry happenings to observe it firsthand for themselves. Try this experiment: Spend several months over-communicating the stories of youth ministry, and see what happens.

Educate your congregation.

In addition to telling youth ministry stories, be clear with people in your congregation about the vital role they play in the overall health of the youth ministry. This may be as simple as saying, "Research shows the congregation's appreciation of students is a significant factor in the overall health of youth ministry in the local church."[57] Most people in most congregations genuinely want students to be involved and connected; they may just need a little encouragement to transition their appreciation from implicit to explicit and move from *informed* to *interested* to *involved* to *intertwined*.

Your pastor can be a huge asset in this area. When my (Tim) pastor is exhorting the congregation to support ministries that may not be automatic homeruns[58] to everyone, he asks the people if they're willing to "give and pray for a ministry you don't like or understand."[59] I think this is a great thing to request that your pastor do to help raise the congregation's appreciation for teenagers.

An incredible organization that is providing top-quality resources for congregations to be better nurturers of adolescents is the Search Institute.[60] Their resources are based on research specific to adolescent health, and they've developed a list of 40 internal and external assets

---

57. In fact, Kara Powell and the Fuller Youth Institute (www.fulleryouthinstitute.org) are engaged in ongoing research that suggests intergenerational connectedness is one of the more significant factors in helping students maintain an active, healthy faith after high school.

58. This is not a book about baseball.

59. Jeff Greenway is a smart dude and great leader who loves God and people.

60. www.search-institute.org

needed by adolescents in order to be healthy. The local church can provide significant help in building these assets, and the Search Institute has developed top-quality, inexpensive resources to help congregations move in that direction. If you're not already familiar with the Search Institute's research, we highly recommend you taking some time to explore their website (www.search-institute.org) and learn how you can help your congregation be asset builders in the lives of adolescents. Go ahead, do it now!

Wave the youth ministry banner to your church staff.

The EYM study found a strong connection between a congregation's appreciation of students and the lead pastor's support of youth ministry. Youth ministry is at its healthiest when the lead pastor understands its value and is committed to its success. When this is occurring, the pastor is communicating support throughout the congregation, both publicly and privately. Lead pastors frequently share these two main complaints about youth ministry: not knowing what's going on in the ministry and covering up for a youth worker's bad decision. Over-communicate with your pastor, and submit yourself to a team that will help you avoid blind spots in your decision-making. If your pastor is not a fan of youth ministry, you're facing a long, uphill battle; help your pastor become a fan by keeping him or her in the communication loop.

While you're at it, keep your entire church staff in the communication loop. Be a team player and coordinate schedules so you're not planning youth events that compete with other complementary programming. Don't keep your church staff in the dark concerning things going on with youth ministry.

You could educate your church staff members on their significance in the dynamic of increasing the congregation's appreciation of students by writing them an executive summary of this and other books that reflect the importance of congregational support. Or (and we say this for no personal gain) you could buy all of your church staff a copy of this book so they can read it for themselves. (OK, maybe there's a little personal gain…very little.)

Work to increase students' appreciation of the congregation.

If we're asking our congregations to appreciate and support youth ministry, it's fair to ask students to appreciate and support the church and its other ministries. And our observation is that many youth workers drop the ball here. Appreciation is a two-way street, and the stages of *involved* and *intertwined* rely on a youth ministry that refuses to be a separate entity.

Part of our discipling of students should help them think past themselves and view themselves as part of the community. Becoming a mature adult means giving, not just taking; becoming a mature youth group means giving, not just taking. As we ask the congregation to support ministries they may not like or understand, we must ask teenagers to do the same.

You should consider bringing the youth group to the puppet show and the Southern Gospel concert. The youth group should have a presence at the next campus workday. Even if students think something is lame, it's healthy to teach them to find value in ministries they don't like or understand. Being a "team player" isn't just a challenge we want to lay before youth workers; we think it is a worthy goal for your youth group as a whole.

One way to help students make this transition is to model it in our own lives. We should never speak negatively about the congregation or leaders in it. We should refrain from joking about things related to the overall church. Instead, we should intentionally speak positively about the congregation, the church leadership, and the church in general. Our attitudes toward the church will manifest in the attitudes of our students.

As we were preparing to write this book, we agreed that this best practice was the one that could pose the most challenges. I (Kurt) have had the wonderful privilege of talking to thousands of youth workers over the years, and the topic of integrating the youth ministry into the life of the church almost always works its way into the conversation. We all recognize the urgency of the issue: Why would teenagers who feel no connection to the larger church body feel comfortable within it after they graduate from the youth group? The answer: They wouldn't. And because that is an unacceptable answer, we hope you will do the hard work required.

For personal reflection:

1. How well do you feel like you are implementing this practice?

    _____ weak

    _____ average

    _____ strong

2. Look again at the stages of congregational appreciation. At what stage is your church currently in?

3. How would you describe the perception your congregation has of your youth ministry?

4. What are a couple of ways you can immediately begin to help your students appreciate your congregation?

Experiential option:

Practice being a team player: Walk the halls of your church, and pray specifically for God's blessings upon its various ministries. Jot down any ideas that come to mind that may help you partner with your colleagues.

BEST PRACTICE

PROVIDE OPPORTUNITIES FOR RELATIONSHIPS

EYM Marker for a Mature Faith:
*Fosters significant relationships and
a sense of community*

It probably comes as no surprise that the subject of providing opportunities for relationships would bubble to the surface of any credible youth ministry discussion. Chances are you have read books, attended seminars, and participated in conversations about the importance of relational youth ministry in its various forms. The EYM study confirms that this is a conversation worth having, so let's talk.

Having relationships with others is a core need that started all the way back when God decided it wasn't good for Adam to be alone. Don't like the idea of relationships? Blame God. The most important relationship is between Creator and creation, and until we are in a proper relationship with our Creator, it's impossible for other relationships to reach their full potential. Yet it isn't easy to develop relationships that reach full potential and fulfill the role God wants them to in our lives; the relationship journey is a minefield with potential danger at every step. And into this minefield walk our students. Few things impact the lives of the teenagers in your youth ministry as much their relationships, so helping them develop healthy relationships is one of the most important and challenging things you do as a youth worker.

Your church is full of great opportunities for young people to develop healthy relationships. To a large degree, the "relationship pool" from which your students can draw will be affected by the relationship your youth ministry has with the rest of the church. To use language from chapter five, think of the difference in potential relationships in an "informed" church versus those in an "intertwined" setting. Obviously a church body in which the congregation and the youth group are intertwined provides the most potential for your students to have a variety of healthy relationships.

Let's look at some of the ways you can help your students develop healthy relationships with others within your church family.

Make it a priority.

Because teenagers are such relational beings, it's easy to assume that everybody in your group feels connected, has healthy friendships, and is known by the adult leaders. Larger youth groups are notorious for seeing large crowds of students at their activities and assuming that it would be impossible for a student to feel disconnected; with so many people in one place, it's impossible not to know somebody! Smaller youth groups make the same mistake; with only a dozen students in the room, it's impossible to feel alone! We wish these statements were true, but they're not.

We were excited to see "providing opportunities for relationships" listed as one of the best practices when we first read through the EYM study, because we think that this is such a "no brainer" for most youth workers that many youth workers put no brainpower into it! Because relationships seem to happen so naturally among our students and because we have relationally minded adults serving with us, it's tempting to spend most of our mental "heavy lifting" on other areas of our ministry. A pitcher's fastball is usually his most developed pitch, but he still throws it over and over in practice.[61] When the "relationship" part of a youth ministry is left to chance, you miss a strategic opportunity. Without any attention, relationships will foster, but they may also quickly begin to fester!

Connect students with adult volunteers.

If you were part of a youth group in junior high or high school, you probably don't remember too many of the lessons. Despite your leader's desperate attempts to make the Bible study times interesting and interactive, we're guessing you have long since forgotten the specifics of virtually every lesson they ever taught. There are exceptions of course, like when Kurt was in high school and his youth worker turned on the overhead projector[62] and asked all the guys to come and sign their names for all to see pledging that they would never again masturbate. Yep, Kurt remembers that one.

While you may not remember the lessons, you probably remember the adults who taught them, and you certainly remember the adults who took the time to get to know you on a more personal level.

---

61. This is not a book about baseball.

62. Overhead projectors were the hot youth group technology of the day. You would lay a "transparency" on its surface, and it would project whatever you wrote on the transparency onto the screen. Some of you may still use these in your setting—and for that, we are sorry!

The two of us do. For me (Tim) it was my youth worker and his wife, Glen and Tylitha Whatley. They were consistent examples of faith and voices of encouragement in my life. Glen spent lots of hours with a small group of guys who felt called to vocational ministry, and when I accepted a call to serve my first church, Tylitha gave solid (and pointed) advice and encouragement. For me (Kurt) it was John Miller in junior high and Doug Heal in high school. John Miller was my Sunday school teacher who showed up at my Pop Warner football games, invited me to meals with his family, and taught me how to ride a dirt bike. Doug Heal was my high school youth worker who took me skiing, saw some leadership potential in me, and gave me opportunities to experiment with my gifts. Though we haven't seen these people in many years, their lives still influence us today.

The impact an adult volunteer can have in the life of an adolescent is huge. I've (Tim) always used this formula, "Caring adults + Teenagers = Good Stuff."[63] It's tough to go wrong when you are helping students connect with caring adults. We'll write more about recruiting and developing committed, competent leadership in chapter seven, but here are a few simple ways you can help students and adult volunteers connect:

1. Make sure every meeting time has some sort of planned connection point—even a small one—between adults and students.

---

63. Kurt actually says this a lot, but I don't want him getting credit for all the pithy statements.

2. Don't allow adult leaders to merely be "chaperones" or the "Sssshhhhhhh!" police. Instead, expect them to sit with teenagers and interact.

3. Train your adult volunteers in the art of being good listeners and good question-askers.

4. Remind your adult volunteers that the best youth ministry happens outside the walls of the church, and empower them to do so.

Don't underestimate the impact OLDER adults can make.

Some of you think an "older adult" is anybody over 40, but since I (Kurt) am in my mid-40s, I would like to differ with that opinion! Yet when I look across the youth ministry landscape, it becomes clear that us old folks often have a hard time finding a youth ministry with a welcome mat that reads: "We Love Old People." If you don't have older adults serving in your youth ministry, you are robbing your students of some very unique relationships. The fact that older adults are less likely to host a sleepover, know all the lyrics to the latest hip-hop song, or hang out at the skate park shouldn't be seen as a liability, but as an opportunity to expose your students to a wonderful group of people who are simply at a different life stage. If you have purposely avoided using older adults as volunteers in your ministry, we would beg you to reconsider.

Some of you welcome the idea but have had trouble convincing older adults to join your team. Our hunch is this is because many older adults feel insecure and wonder what they have to offer since they don't want to host a sleepover, don't know the lyrics to the latest hip-hop song, and have no desire to hang out at the skate park. If they've ever taken the time to think about what they do offer, those thoughts may have quickly been hijacked by thoughts of what they don't offer. Ask some of the older adults in your congregation if they've ever considered serving in your youth ministry, and I'll (Tim) bet Kurt's share of the proceeds of this book that part of their answer will include their own insecurities.[64]

What can we do?

First, we can acknowledge and work through our own baggage and doubts about older adults. Sometimes older adults scare us. (There, we said it.) Many of us unfortunately have good reasons to be afraid: We've been burned by older adults in our pasts. We hear you, and we understand. But we also want to encourage you to do the work it takes to move forward. Don't make the healthy older adults in your congregation pay for the unhealthy older adults from your past.

Some of you are probably pushing back in this section. You may be saying something like: "Whoa, fellas. I don't have the issues you're discussing; I just wonder if older adults are relevant to students. I wonder if older adults will mess up what I've been building in our student ministry by being boring or old-fashioned." Isn't God bigger than this? Can't God use older adults to be more effective than we are in ministering with teenagers? Maybe some older adults wouldn't make good volunteers, but couldn't we say the same thing about younger adults? We need to use

---

64. I'm not offering a subtle commentary about gambling. I'm just making a joke, which Kurt tells me is not funny if I have to explain it.

good discernment as we recruit volunteers, but let's decide not to let age be a filter we apply to our recruiting.

A few years ago, 77-year-old John Allen walked into our junior high meeting space and declared, "God woke me up last night and told me to work with junior highers." Because I (Kurt) was raised to respect my elders, I figured elders who get awakened by God in the middle of the night deserved an extra measure of respect! So we let John join our volunteer team, and his time with us was one of the best seasons our ministry has ever experienced. John learned names quicker than anybody I've ever been around, and he loved stationing himself by our doors and greeting students as they came in. John has recently left our team to help take care of his ailing girlfriend (yes, you read that right…girlfriend!), and he has left a hole in our ministry that will be tough to fill. It would have been so easy to let my preconceived notions of senior adults keep me from embracing John's desire to work with junior highers, and I'm so glad I didn't let that happen.

Second, we can ask specific older adults in our congregations if they would consider getting involved with student ministry. We must be specific in what we're asking them to do: chaperone lock-ins, greet students as they enter our meeting space, or coach a small group. These older adults have concerns that younger adults rarely consider: health, energy, the impact of youth ministry on their dentures, and so on. It's helpful if we spell out the day and time commitment up front and give them an opportunity to say no if needed. If you're struggling to identify older adults who might be a good fit with your youth ministry, ask your students. One or more students usually have a relationship with an older adult; let the students help you make your list of "targets." (They should be easy targets to hit, since they don't move very fast.)

Third, we can ask groups of older adults for input on how to help connect them with teenagers. Lee is an older adult who teaches senior high Sunday school in my (Tim) church. During a volunteer meeting early in my ministry at this church, I shared my commitment to helping students and older adults connect. Lee hung around until other volunteers had left and asked me what I had in mind. I told him I really didn't know, but I wanted to figure out something. He told me that in a recent gathering of older adults, several in their group expressed an interest in connecting with the youth ministry. They kicked some ideas around, including a mentoring program, and asked Lee if he would talk to me about it. God was opening the hearts of these older adults toward students. I wonder if God is doing the same thing in your church? Who might be a few older adults you can speak with?

Last, we can look for ways to help teenagers connect with older adults outside of the youth ministry setting. Encourage students to sit near older adults during corporate gatherings and events; encourage older adults to be approachable and welcoming. Look for ways your youth ministry can serve the older adults in your congregation. Can they target an older couple who needs help with yard work? Is there a widow who could use some help? Can your students serve at the annual senior adult Christmas banquet? Spend some of your creative energy thinking through a good way to bridge the generational gap, and help teenagers connect with those who have journeyed a little further down life's path.

Connect students with each other.

Ask your students why they're a part of a church community, and one of the top answers will have something to do with friendships. In fact, a recent survey of 10,000 Christian teenagers conducted by GROUP Magazine, kids were asked to identify what was most important in their youth group experience. Number one: "A welcoming atmosphere where I can be myself." Number two: "Quality relationships." Many youth workers view teenagers' desire for friendships as a part of youth ministry that has been over-emphasized, resulting in a generation of "shallow" Christians. Instead of wishing these findings away, it may be wise to embrace them! God made humans to need one another, and adolescents are no exception to this truth. Consider this sample of the more than 30 "one another" commands in the New Testament:

Be devoted to one another in brotherly love. Honor one another above yourselves (Romans 12:10 NIV).

Be kind and compassionate to one another, forgiving each other, just as in Christ God forgave you (Ephesians 4:32 NIV).

Encourage one another daily… (Hebrews 3:13 NIV).

If God didn't create us to be deeply connected to one another, why did he tell us in so much detail how to relate to one another? Because adolescents are moving toward decreased dependence on their parents, the need becomes even greater for them to connect with other healthy students in order to journey well through life.

How cool is it when a student leads another student to faith in Christ? Or when a student walks another student toward maturity? Or when a group of students begin to hold one another accountable? God wired students to help one another through the spiritual formation process; they just need a little training. A youth worker friend often tells his students, "You should always be reaching back to help someone on their journey, reaching forward to accept help from others, and reaching up to connect with God, and allow God to hold it together."[65]

It is rare that any of what we mentioned above happens by accident. Not too many teenage friendships take on this type of flavor, not because students aren't open to it or able to go there, but because they don't typically go there without some encouragement and coaching. By default, the students in your youth group are connecting with each other, but are they connecting in a way that is much different than how they would connect with each other if they weren't part of a youth ministry? Is it really possible? We think it is!

Embrace the power of small groups.

We don't think any of you are surprised by seeing a section in this book dedicated to small groups. Call them what you like: Sunday school, Life Groups, Journey Groups, Cell Groups, Core Groups, Care Groups, or even something super cool like Communional Groups[66], but at this moment in the history of youth ministry, it would be tough to find a

---

65. For the life of me, I (Tim) can't remember who said this to me. Whoever you are, if you're reading this book, e-mail us at timandkurtrippedmeoff@gmail.com and we'll say a hearty "Thank you!"

66. In his book *Youth Ministry 3.0*, Mark Oestreicher uses the phrase "communional" to paint a new picture of what youth ministry might look like. Haven't read *Youth Ministry 3.0*? You need to.

youth group that isn't utilizing small groups in some fashion. And for good reason: Encouraging teenagers to regularly share life in a smaller setting with peers they have grown to trust and a caring adult cheering them on is a potent proposition!

Small group proponents (of which we are two) often struggle with several issues that we agree are important to reconcile. First, you may have heard the distinction between "a church *of* small groups" and "a church *with* small groups." The difference may seem insignificant, but settling on an answer will help you process the rest of the questions. In a church *of* small groups, the central part of life in the body is the small group. In a church *with* small groups, the life of the body is experienced equally in multiple ways, including small groups. Both views have pros and cons, and (probably with some input from your church leadership) you need to think through which approach is best in your youth ministry. Both of us view our settings as "a church with small groups." Small groups are a very important part of our church (and student ministry) experiences, but they exist within a more traditional church structure.

A second issue is to determine the purpose of small groups. Are they outreach-focused, employing the "empty chair" philosophy (the act of setting an empty chair in the circle each meeting and asking students who they might invite next week to "fill the empty chair")? Are they discipleship-intensive groups that emphasize spiritual growth? Are they social groups that gather to watch the new episode of their favorite TV show? Are they affinity-based groups that gather around a shared interest? We think it's easier to pick a purpose and philosophy and apply it to all of your small groups, but easier isn't always better. We have heard of youth ministries that have a variety of small group options to meet the needs of a variety of students. It takes quite a bit of extra effort, but perhaps making the small group experience relevant to as many students as possible is worth it.

Another issue is about the location of the small groups. Should they meet on the church campus? Should they meet in members' homes? Is it OK for the leader of the group to also host it? What about meeting in a restaurant or coffee shop? How about on a school campus? This issue may seem a bit less significant philosophically, but the location of the groups will shape the outcomes, so choose wisely.[67] We have seen small groups work in every setting imaginable, and we've seen groups flounder because they are in the wrong setting. It's important to decide what you hope to accomplish during your small group time and choose a location that best sets you up to win.

All of this is worth your consideration, but don't let any of the details of small groups get in the way of the real purpose: relationships— specifically building authentic community. If your group is evangelistic, you are doing evangelism in community. If your group is focused on discipleship, you are doing spiritual formation in community. If you're watching TV, you're enjoying media in community. Sometimes we feel guilty if we focus on the relational piece of small groups, as if focusing on evangelism or discipleship is more important. If the relationship piece weren't important, why would you organize into small groups in the

---

67. Read with Robert Eddison's British accent, a la the Grail Knight in *Indiana Jones and the Last Crusade.*

first place? If all youth ministry needed was large gatherings, why would phrases like "grow larger and smaller at the same time" become clichés? As you wrestle through these issues, don't allow the primary strength of small groups—relationships—to become secondary.

Build relationships through missions and other service projects.

Some of most significant spiritual experiences I (Tim) had as a teenager were in Estherwood, Louisiana, on mission trips. Like most youth group mission trips, ours were a combination of ministering to kids and building something. The first time I participated, I had been a follower of Christ for less than a year, and I had no idea what to expect. I knew I was going to help people, and I was excited for the opportunity. What I didn't realize was how much I would benefit from the experience. I went to give, and I received. I went to teach, and I learned. I went to serve, and God served me. And I certainly wasn't the only one who had such wonderful experiences; virtually every student on every trip I went on had similar stories. I'm sure it would have been a good experience had I been by myself, but it was a great experience because I lived it with my brothers and sisters in faith.

Remember when we described *communitas* in chapter three? (We'll wait for you to do a little review.) *Communitas* is the deeper connection a group develops when its members experience a shakeup of normal living. Perhaps this is why retreats and camps are so impacting—they allow students' normal daily schedules to be interrupted. Mission projects allow for the shakeup of normal living by the intentional choice of doing something for someone else—living and revealing the kingdom of God.

Mission and service projects allow relationships in your group to develop more quickly because the participants' schedules are disrupted. From serving several hours in a soup kitchen to a 14-day trip to Africa, mission projects rip us out of our normal lives and thrust us into the reality of God's presence as we give ourselves away, and *communitas* is developed. *Communitas* will help keep teenagers connected to each other and to their faith long after their high school education comes to an end.

How to do it? Plan service projects with your students regularly. Go clean up a local park and playground. Call a local school and offer to repaint as needed. Maintain a senior adult's yard. Sort clothes for a clothes pantry. Work in a soup kitchen. Sing at a nursing home. Offer free children's story times at a local library. Adopt a child through Compassion International.[68] Serve in a foreign country. Do something—anything— for someone else. Get students out of their comfort zones and allow *communitas* to develop as they serve together.[69]

Celebrate the cliques in your group.

Carrie, a high school junior, flopped down in the chair across from my (Tim) desk and sighed. When I looked up from my computer, I could see the angst on her face. With gravity in her voice, she lowered the boom: "We have cliques in our youth group." I breathed a huge sigh of relief, because I was worried she was going to tell me something bad I didn't know.

---

68. www.compassion.com

69. One more shout out to the Search Institute (www.search-institute.org) for the book *Beyond Leaf Raking*, by Peter Benson and Eugene Roehlkepartain (1993). They've released some updated editions, but the original has a certain charm that we find appealing. They've also developed a partner website—www.servicelearning.org—filled with practical ideas on how to mobilize students to service and build communitas.

She noticed my relief and asked, "Shouldn't you be worried about that? Aren't you going to say something?" I smiled, thought for a few seconds, and said, "Yes. Next week, we'll talk about cliques."

The following Sunday, I taught a Bible study called, "Celebrate Your Cliques." I asked students to list all the cliques in their schools and ascribe a percentage of their schools' populations to each group. Then I asked students to put a star by the clique they're most often associated with. And for the next 15 minutes, we talked about the opportunity to live and reveal the kingdom within those groups—those cliques to which we already belong.

We totally understand why youth workers want to break up cliques in their youth groups. Cliques can cause hurt feelings of alienation and distrust, they can make people feel excluded and isolated, and they can create a closed climate in your group that's hard for outsiders to break into. But do cliques have to operate that way? Can cliques be redeemed and their powers used for forces of good rather than evil? We think they can!

God created us as relational beings that need close friends. God also created us as unique individuals with highly differentiated likes, strengths, and gifts. Perhaps incarnational living in our youth groups means going into the groups we're already a part of—our cliques—to live and reveal the kingdom of God. Maybe we do students harm when we teach them to lose their individuality and become like everyone else.

For years, I (Kurt) was convinced that we needed to make the "breaking down of cliques" a goal in our youth ministry. I was totally OK with the concept of affinity-based ministries and small groups, yet I was opposed to cliques. I'm a slow learner, and nobody has ever accused me of being the smartest guy in the room, which is why it took me so long to recognize that I had really just been playing a semantics game. I wasn't opposed to students clumping together with others who had similar interests ("affinity"); I was just opposed to the ugliness that often resulted (how I defined "cliques"). For me, a change of attitude was as simple as changing my working definition of the word "cliques."

I like the way Tim's youth group fought against exclusive cliques. They instituted the five-minute rule.[70] Every time his youth group gathers, students are asked to spend the first five minutes after they arrive and the first five minutes after the program is over to connect with people they don't already know. It's OK to grab a buddy and work the room as a pair, but they want students getting out of their closed circle of friends and making room for new and/or disconnected students to join. To help them remember, the adult volunteers will randomly shout, "Remember the five-minute rule!" as teenagers trickle into the meeting space. And the upfront person will say the same thing as the program comes to an end. Little things like the five-minute rule will help keep the ugly side of cliques from bubbling to the surface.

---

70. I (Tim) can't remember if I made this up or if I ripped it off from someone else. If this was your idea, please e-mail us at timandkurtrippedmeoff@gmail.com and we'll say a hearty "Thank you!"

Cut back on cutdowns.

You may have heard the statistic that reported 80 percent of the things teenagers say are negative. We spent some time searching for the source of that statement and couldn't find anything. But when we've thrown that number out to teenagers, they've often disagreed; they believe the statistic is actually *higher*—that more of what they say is negative! Then they call us stupid idiots for not already knowing this.

Have you ever wondered how that affects a youth group?

In case teenagers don't hear enough negative things at school, at work, or at home, they're also hearing it when they gather with their youth group! Youth groups are a hotbed of cutdowns, ridicule, gossip, and poking fun at others…and that's just what the adult leaders are doing! I (Kurt) have the spiritual gift of sarcasm; seriously, I am really good at it and use it quite often. I also have an impressive record of getting a laugh at the expense of somebody else. Over the years I have been on a journey. I used to let the sarcastic, and very funny, jabs fly without a hint of remorse because certainly everybody knew I was joking and if they were bothered, they needed to get thicker skin. Next, I decided if I knowingly offended someone or hurt somebody's feelings, I would seek that person out to apologize after the fact. This was a perfect plan because I could get the laugh up front, then feel good about myself for making amends later on. Today I am working on eliminating sarcasm and hurtful humor altogether. It isn't easy, but my "I think I need to go apologize to so and so" rate has dropped significantly!

Negative words are powerful weapons, and unfortunately most youth groups are armed like a Montana militia![71] Using words as a weapon of mass destruction instead of tools for edification and encouragement may be the biggest hindrance to true community in your youth group. Think about this for a moment: Authentic community is fostered best where there is safety, trust, security, and freedom. When teenagers are afraid to be themselves for fear of being picked on, or hesitant to share their thoughts for fear of being ridiculed, or generally feel like others are quick on the draw with a sharp word, why would they ever take the risk of sharing a genuine hurt, fear, or struggle?

So what do you do? Well, if it's true that more than 80 percent of what teenagers have to say is negative, maybe the first thing to do is recognize that we have an uphill battle! Perhaps the second thing to do is pray for God's wisdom to help you combat the culture of cutdowns, and maybe a third thing to do is start with yourself.

Before you push back and tell us we're being too nitpicky, let us share a thought from Paul. The Bible is full of wisdom when it comes to our words, and we think this is one of the more compelling nuggets:

When you talk, do not say harmful things, but say what people need—words that will help others become stronger. Then what you say will do good to those who listen to you (Ephesians 4:29 NCV).

---

71. Kurt wrote that, and it's a joke at the expense of the good folks from Montana. Way to go, Kurt.

We tried (Kurt really tried!), but we still haven't found a biblical precedence for teasing. The more we looked, the more obvious it became that God's ideal is for his followers to use their words to build up, not tear down, those he so dearly loves.

Consider developing a mentoring plan.

We confess that neither of us has a formal mentoring plan in place in our churches. We hope it happens naturally, and we believe to some degree it is. But if we were honest, we'd admit that it doesn't happen as much as we'd like. Our lack of adoption of a mentoring program doesn't diminish the reality that it is a fantastic way to build deep, life changing, relationships. It's challenging, time-consuming, and frustrating—and it's rewarding, kingdom-building, and worth it.

Loads of research confirms the positive effects of mentoring on adolescents. From the U.S. Department of Education, to the Big Brothers Big Sisters of America, to Christ-centered groups like the Christian Association of Youth Mentoring, numerous organizations have confirmed the significant impact adults have on teenagers' lives through mentoring. I (Tim) have a youth ministry buddy serving in an urban setting, and after repeated attempts to build a healthy youth ministry, he shifted his focus and rebuilt his ministry around mentoring relationships. As I was researching for this book, he told me that the relationships students and mentors develop have been the driving force for young people in his community to avoid at-risk behaviors and pursue higher goals.

Because neither of us is doing this well, we are hesitant to write much more about it. But certainly when thinking about the power of relationships and the best practice of providing opportunities for healthy relationships to flourish, a formal mentoring program is worth consideration. If you would like to mentor us on the ways of mentoring, please feel free![72]

Relationships happen. Your youth ministry is a wonderful place to make sure they happen well!

For personal reflection:

1. How well do you feel like you are implementing this practice?

_____ weak

_____ average

_____ strong

2. How open are you to the idea of older adults serving on your team? How might you continue to encourage older adults to join your efforts?

---

72. The *Be-With Factor* by Bo Boshers, *Jesus-Centered Youth Ministry* by Rick Lawrence, and *Mentoring from Start to Finish* from Simply Youth Ministry have some good mentoring nuggets.

3. There's nothing new about small groups, but did anything new come to mind while reading this chapter?

4. What cliques exist in your youth ministry? What can you do to celebrate them and keep them headed in a positive direction?

Experiential option:

Consider having a "jab jar" in your youth room. Every time a student or leader is caught choosing words poorly, they have to put a quarter in the "jab jar." Tim tried this and raised enough money for a 15-passenger van in a month! (OK, it was closer to raising enough money for a pizza party in a year.)

BEST PRACTICE

DEVELOP CONFIDENT, COMPETENT, AND COMMITTED ADULT LEADERS

EYM Marker for a Mature Faith:
The ministry is developing committed, competent leaders

We've all heard the saying, "There are no lone rangers in youth ministry"—that healthy leaders understand the importance of building a team. The EYM study shows that this age-old saying is as true today as it was when the Lone Ranger recruited Tonto.

John Maxwell is known for the phrase, "Everything rises and falls on leadership."[73] You don't have to be a John Maxwell fan to recognize the truth of that simple statement. Virtually everyone who has served in youth ministry has stories of wonderfully committed and competent adults who were a vital part of what God was doing among their students. And virtually everyone has horror stories of the damage done by adult leaders who should never have been allowed to oversee students in the first place. If everything rises and falls on leadership, it would be wise to consider what type of leaders are serving alongside you and what you can do to help increase their confidence, competence, and commitment.[74]

---

73. Most people agree that John Maxwell said this first.

74. Although we are emphasizing "adult leaders" in this chapter, we believe strongly in the importance and power of developing student leaders as well.

Too often, youth workers spend almost all of their time, resources, and energy on ministry with students and give the leftovers to their adult leaders. A healthier balance might be spending one-third of your time, resources, and energy with students, one-third with families, and one-third with adult volunteers. As we explore leadership development in this chapter, keep this time distribution in mind because building a team of confident, competent, and committed adult volunteers doesn't happen without your willingness to put some skin in the game.[75]

We initially set out to structure this chapter in a way that cleanly articulated some tips under each category of "confidence," "competence," and "commitment," but we quickly realized that these three areas work together—one breeds the other which breeds the next, and this happens in a different order for different people. So instead of compartmentalizing our thoughts, we have lumped them all together.

Build wisely.

If everything rises and falls on leadership, then you need to be very wise when building your team of leaders. Build wisely, and you'll free yourself to focus on finding the next batch of quality leaders. Build unwisely, and eventually you'll have to make staff changes to correct your mistakes. Here are a few short thoughts you may find interesting as you begin building your team:

- Your ministry is probably desperate for leaders, but it isn't desperate for the wrong ones.

---

75. This is not a book about baseball.

- It's easier to say "no" to a potential leader than to try to remove them later.

- Don't say somebody's "no" for them (in other words, don't be afraid to ask an adult to join your team because you assume that person won't be interested).[76]

- You have not because you ask not. Get aggressive—your youth group is awesome, and people need to be part of it!

Because it is so important to build the right team of leaders, you need to put a few things in place to help ensure this happens. Here is a short list of things to include that will help you add the right players to your team:[77]

- Create a formal application for potential leaders to fill out. Include questions that you deem important for you to know about an adult volunteer.[78] Ask each potential volunteer for two letters of recommendation from other members of your church.

- Ask each potential volunteer to submit to fingerprinting or a formal background check.[79]

---

76. Bill Hybels is known to say this quite a bit.

77. This is not a book about baseball.

78. www.churchvolunteercentral.com is a "one-stop shop" for this sort of stuff.

79. For a great background check option visit www.churchvolunteercentral.com.

- When the application, recommendation letters, and background check are complete, schedule a formal interview with the potential volunteer.

- If, after the interview, both parties feel like moving forward, invite the potential volunteer to observe your youth group in action.

- Have a follow-up meeting to discuss next steps.

It takes time to build a confident, competent, and committed team of adults. Don't give into the pressure you feel to quickly load up with any breathing adult willing to help out; your ministry to teenagers is too important to take shortcuts.

Eliminate some of their fears.

The idea of working with teenagers is unsettling to most adults. When adults enter a room full of students, their first thoughts are usually along these lines: "Will they like me?" "Am I too old?" "Is my zipper down?"

One of the top concerns adults have when considering working with students is, "Am I relevant?" They may not articulate it that way, but they're thinking it and feeling it. Adult volunteers are funny animals, and they respond to the relevancy issue differently. Some try to be super hip, changing the way they dress and talk to relate to students. Others try to be comedians, constantly cracking jokes and making light of everything. Still others try to be super spiritual, feeling compelled to know all the answers to every question students ask. We believe many of these responses come out of our adult volunteers' own insecurities. It's important to recognize that for many adults, the teenage years were horrific and the thought of reliving them is…well, it's something they don't want to think about. Part of your role is to help the adults on your team work through these issues in a healthy way.

One of the best gifts you can give your adult leaders is the freedom to be themselves. Help them recognize they have something to offer that your students desperately need. God wired them uniquely and wants to use them to make a unique impact in your youth ministry. Let's look at this concept a little closer.

Help adults serve where they TILT.

For much of my ministry career, I (Kurt) consistently made the same strategic error when it came to placing volunteer leaders in ministry roles on our junior high team. Because I was intimately aware of every single leadership hole and role that needed to be filled, I would quickly plug new leaders into whatever hole or role that currently needed to be filled. If we were short on small group leaders, new recruits became small group leaders; if we were short on weekend leaders, new recruits became weekend leaders; and if we were short on office help, new recruits became folders of paper and stuffers of envelopes.

All the while I kept finding myself puzzled over the fact that so many of our volunteers who only months earlier were beaming with enthusiasm would suddenly decide that junior high ministry wasn't for them. And all the while I kept finding myself talking to these leaders about their experience and asking them if there was a reason for their sudden departure. What I learned surprised me. And what surprises me even more is how long it took for what I learned to impact the way I helped volunteer leaders find their role within our ministry.

The key word in the last sentence is "helped." You see, I had never really helped leaders at all; in fact, I viewed them as people who were there to help me, and I simply plopped them into a ministry role that would help me the best. I'm a pretty sharp leader, so after losing several dozen volunteers by making the same mistake over and over again, I figured something needed to change. When I shifted my focus from "How can they help me minister to students?" to "How can I help them minister to students?" things suddenly began to change. I answered the question "How can I help them minister to students?" by freeing them up to serve where they naturally tilted.

Everyone tilts toward certain aspects of your youth ministry, and the direction they tilt has to do with the way God has wired them, their life experiences, and other factors. To help my volunteer team members discover how they tilt, I created a "TILT Test" (original, I know). After working through the TILT Test together, we release our volunteers to serve in an area of ministry that seems like the best fit. Often it isn't an area that I need help in the most, but because it is in an area of their choosing based on how they TILT, our volunteer leaders stay involved much longer than in years past.

Here's how the TILT Test works :

The first part of discovering how people tilt is to help them identify some of what makes them unique.

- **Tools:** Everybody brings tools to the youth ministry table. These tools include spiritual gifts and natural and learned abilities.

- **Inclinations:** Everybody has certain inclinations. Some are inclined to be reserved, while others are inclined to be outgoing. Some are inclined to be organized, while others are inclined to be spontaneous. Some are inclined to be critical thinkers, while others are inclined to be creative thinkers.

- **Loves:** Everybody has certain "loves" and passions. These are the things that have captured your heart. Loves cover everything from hobbies to movies to charitable causes to social issues and beyond. Everybody has some things they love.

- **Total life experience:** Everybody has a different life journey, and this life journey has impacted each person dramatically.

While what follows is really the "meat" of the TILT test and can stand alone without the above portion, I think helping your volunteers learn a little bit more about themselves will help bring clarity to what they discover in this next part. I recommend using the two portions together.

The second part of discovering how people tilt involves the process of identifying how they feel about various roles within your ministry. One of my goals is to try to ensure that adults who join my ministry team are spending more and more time doing things they like and are good at, and less and less time doing other things. Virtually every role volunteers might be asked to play will fall into one of four categories for them:

They will like it and be good at it; they will be good at it, but not like it; they will like it, but not be good at it; or they will neither like it nor be good at it. I want my volunteer leaders to serve in an area that leaves them feeling both fruitful and fulfilled (fruitful meaning they are effective in their role, and fulfilling meaning it brings about a sense of purpose and joy). The TILT chart (Diagram 1) will help your leaders discover what areas in your ministry are most likely to provide a fruitful and fulfilling ministry experience.

Diagram 1

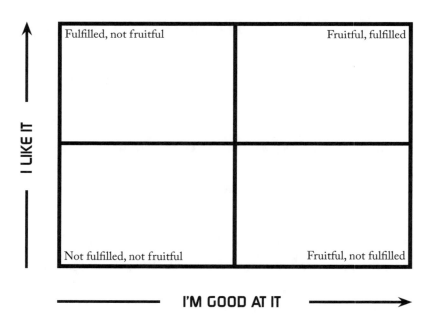

By providing potential volunteers a list of questions related to various opportunities within your ministry and asking them to plot their feelings toward each question on the TILT chart, you can begin to identify what ministry roles they naturally tilt toward. Start by identifying the major categories of opportunity within your ministry, and assign each category a letter. Then write a dozen or so statements that loosely relate to each category. Give each volunteer a blank TILT chart and a list of the statements, and ask them to plot their response to each question based on to what degree they feel like they "like" and "are good at" what the statement is describing. Below are some sample categories:

- LARGE GROUP LEADER (A)

- SMALL GROUP LEADER (B)

- HELPING STUDENTS GROW IN THEIR FAITH (C)

- COACHING ADULTS/LEADING OTHER LEADERS (D)

- SPECIAL EVENTS (E)

- SERVING BEHIND THE SCENES (F)

And here are some sample statements:

- Helping run games (a)

- Spending time with a hurting student (c)

- Organizing activities (e)

- Making phone calls (f)

- Greeting new students (a)

- Leading a Bible study (b)

- Teaching a lesson (a)

- Encouraging other adult leaders (d)

- Interviewing potential volunteers (e)

- Hosting a group of students in your home (b)

- Attending a sporting event of a student (b)

- Being around large crowds of students, many of whom are un-churched (e)

- Mentoring a student (c)

- Clerical work (f)

- Grabbing a coffee after work with another adult leader (d)

Diagram 2 shows what a TILT chart might look like after the statements have plotted.

Diagram 2

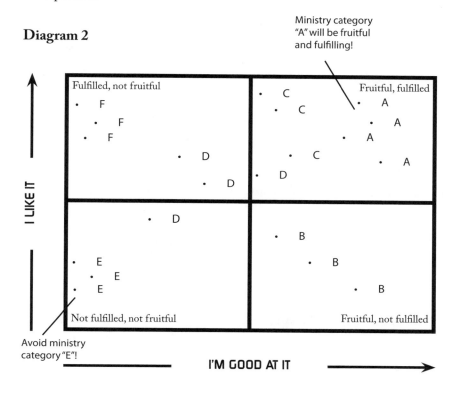

Ministry category "A" will be fruitful and fulfilling!

You will notice that certain letters tend to cluster together in one of the four quadrants. When a certain letter clusters in the "I like it, and I'm good at it" quadrant, that indicates that it is category of ministry that will likely result in a fruitful and fulfilling experience. Plug your volunteer into that category! When a certain letter clusters in the "I don't like it, and I'm not good at it" quadrant, that indicates that it is a category that will likely result in a non-fruitful, non-fulfilling experience. Don't plug a person into that category!

The quadrant that holds the most potential is "fruitful and fulfilled." Next is "fulfilled, but not fruitful." Why? When people like something, they can often, with a little coaching, begin to see positive results. The ministry categories that are found clustered in these two quadrants are worth pursuing with that particular volunteer.

Avoid placing volunteers in ministry roles that fall into the other two quadrants. If people don't like something and aren't good at it, why would you ask them to serve in that area? Sadly, far too many people spend their lives working at careers that would fall into the "I don't like it, but I'm good at it" quadrant. How many times have you heard somebody say something like, "I wish I could change jobs, but I have a mortgage to pay," or, "I hate my job, but I'm good at it; besides, what else would I do?" We call these people the widget-makers; they hate making widgets, but they are good at it, and making widgets pays the bills. Because we would never wish that scenario on people in the workforce, why would we ask them to minister to students in a similar scenario?

We believe something serendipitous happens when we help adults who love God and like students find roles in our ministries in which they excel and that they enjoy: Everyone wins! Students win because leaders stick around longer and enjoy their role. Leaders win because ministry becomes fruitful and fulfilling. Youth workers win because their volunteers are serving where they naturally tilt and finding success in the process and as a result are staying on board for years instead of weeks. And parents win because other adults are joyfully pouring into their children.

Expand the box.

A few years ago, I (Tim) called Kurt for some advice in working with a particularly hardheaded adult volunteer I had inherited from the previous youth worker's tenure. Let's call the volunteer Sheila. She had a good heart for students, but she wasn't executing her responsibilities well. Sheila unintentionally could be abrupt in her tone of voice, and she was blind to it. Plus, she was resistant to any coaching or training. I'm sure none of you can relate....

During one especially challenging "truth in love" conversation, Sheila was getting frustrated at my suggestions on different ways she could do some things. At one point in the exchange, she asked, "Why are you micromanaging me?" I don't think Sheila realized it, but she had just pushed one of my buttons. I remember driving home from our meeting with these thoughts in my head, "I don't think I'm micromanaging her... but am I? No, I'm not. I owe it to the students to hold Sheila to the same standards of excellence as the rest of the volunteers. But maybe I'm pushing her too hard...maybe I should back off a bit and let her figure it out on her own. But what if she doesn't make any changes? What if she keeps things just as they are now?"

So I called Kurt, told him the story, and he spoke some of the most profound words of leadership development ever uttered by mortal man. After a reflective moment of rumination, Kurt broke the silence and said (and I quote), "Dude, you've got to give people freedom, just not freedom to suck." In other words, we want to empower leaders and give them lots of freedom within their roles, but not so much freedom that we set them up to fail. Those hallowed (or maybe hollow?) words have become part of the foundation and framework for my adult volunteer philosophy. At that moment I realized that in some areas, I needed to continue to give Sheila freedom, while in other areas, I needed to reel her in.

You have a decision to make. Do you want to run a ministry in which you hold onto everything tightly with lots of protocol, policy, and policing of who is doing what, where, with whom, and under whose approval? Or do you want to run a ministry that allows ministry to run free, unencumbered by unnecessary control and regulation? Not sure which way you should answer? Let us give you a hint: YOU WANT THE SECOND OPTION! The second option unleashes what we like to call the power of expanding the box. Let us explain.

Much has been made about the importance of providing leaders with well-defined, easily evaluated roles or job descriptions. Conventional wisdom says that ministry happens best when everybody has a clean and clear role, with clean and clear objectives, under a clean and clear chain of command, and within a clean and clear set of guidelines. The thinking is that when the ministry and those who are leading within it are packaged together in a nice, safe box, good things will happen. Or more importantly, nothing bad will happen!

But the truth is there is very little within youth ministry that is clean and clear! There is no such thing as a nice, safe box! Youth ministry is fluid, and things you can count on one minute often vanish into thin air the next. We don't think eliminating "the box" entirely is a good idea; there is a place for structure. But we do think your ministry to students will be much more vibrant when you "expand the box" of your adult leaders and let them think creatively about their roles, set some goals of their own, make important decisions, and do a whole bunch of stuff that is usually reserved for the youth ministry point person.

We suggest you minimize the amount of stuff you put in the "box" of your volunteers. Only include the non-negotiable items so there is plenty of space for them to add stuff of their own, thus expanding the box and allowing ministry to flourish.

This isn't proposing a lack of concern or quality control on your part. Remember Kurt's words of wisdom: "You've got to give people freedom, just not freedom to suck." If you choose to experience the power of expanding the box, you will need to dedicate yourself to paying attention to all the moving parts of your youth ministry and helping your leaders navigate their freedom wisely. But the result will be a team of adult volunteers who feel trusted and empowered to literally think outside the box!

This begs the question, "What do I do if my volunteers want clear guidelines and lots of direction?" Give it to them. Most adults spend the vast majority of their time working and performing under their employers' rules, regulations, and expectations, so it makes sense they would feel more comfortable in a similar ministry setting. The beauty of expanding the box is that it is both a tangible concept you can put into practice AND a philosophy you can slowly allow people to warm up to.

Share life before you share your expertise.

Training is an important part of building a confident, competent, and committed team. But don't make the mistake of assuming that a well-trained team is automatically a good team. The sports history books are full of baseball teams that looked good on paper but come game time couldn't seem to function together well.[80] The same is true with youth ministry teams in churches all across the country. Our advice? Focus on building chemistry more than on training skills.

I (Kurt) currently serve in a very large ministry environment—my youth ministry team consists of almost 300 adult leaders, dozens of whom have served for 10 years or more. Ask any of the long-term veterans why they've stuck it out so long, and they will usually answer something along these lines: "I feel like the youth ministry team is my church family," or, "Well, I like teenagers, but I absolutely love being on the youth ministry team," or, "Kurt comes to my house and washes my car every Saturday."

None of this has happened by accident. We have discovered that if you focus on sharing life and building community among your adult volunteers, they will stick around for a while and you will have plenty of time to train them. Because of this we work hard to build a sense of community among our leaders that helps them understand that we care more about them as friends than we do about their role as a leader.

But formal training is a vital part of helping your leaders grow in confidence, competence, and commitment. So what do you do?

---

80. This is not a book about baseball.

Tim and I differ in our approach to training our adults. Tim favors a more formal, structured, and systematic approach, while I like being a bit more informal and organic. (This is interesting considering the fact that Tim is a laid-back, longhaired, emerging sort of leader, while I tend to be a bit more driven, pragmatic, and bald). Tim likes to have monthly team meetings while I prefer to meet quarterly. Tim employs a more formal evaluation process while I prefer to get a "feel" for how things are going. But while we differ in *how* we train, we are very similar in *what* we train.

Here are a handful of topics we think are important:

1. **Youth ministry overview.** An overview of your youth ministry's goals, values, programs, mission statement, and "core essentials." Make sure your leaders know what way your youth group is headed, and be clear in your expectation that they must head in the same direction.

2. **The "Dirty Half-Dozen."** This is a short but important list of six non-negotiables your leaders need to adhere to. Some examples:

   • Never be alone with a student of the opposite sex.

   • Never undermine the authority of a parent.

   • Never promise a student you can keep a secret.

- Always share with the youth worker any reports of abuse, illegal activity, and other serious issues so he/she can take appropriate next steps.

- Never use any form of physical punishment.

- Never allow students to bully or haze others.

3. **Understanding youth culture.** You could probably repeat this one quarterly with new and valid insights. Walt Mueller's Center for Parent/Youth Understanding (www.cpyu.org) is a great place to start. For an unfiltered (sometimes rough language and always candid honesty) adolescent perspective, consider SpankMag! (www.spankmag.com).

4. **Counseling students.** At some point, most adult volunteers will have a teenager ask them for advice. Help your adults filter through what is and is not appropriate for them to counsel.

5. **Putting yourself in their shoes.** Work your leaders through an exercise that takes them back in time to their own teenage years. As teenagers, what were their struggles, fears, hopes, parental issues, and other big issues?

6. **Preparing a Bible study (and/or leading a small group).** Often the things we take for granted are the things most needed by our adult volunteers.

7. Social networking with students. We still believe one of the most powerful things adults can give students is their presence—at sporting events, dance recitals, concerts, family gatherings, and so on—but social networking allows them unprecedented connection points with students that should be utilized.

You may have heard the saying, "It's not what you say; it's what you emphasize." You can find some great resources—for free or for a fee—on training your adult volunteers, and we would encourage you to review them and find some good stuff to share with your leaders. But what are you emphasizing with your adults? We encourage you to do some serious thinking and reflecting on your youth group and your context and articulate a few key principles you want to address regularly with your adult volunteers. Here are a few we like to include:

- You don't have to be cool; you just have to be real. Don't pretend to have it all together; be transparent and vulnerable.

- Students are not looking for a superstar that has it all figured out; they're looking for someone to whom they can relate who is doing their best to live a life of God's kingdom.

- It's OK to speak honestly and appropriately about your doubts and your struggles.[81] And it's OK not to have all the answers.

---

81. Adults need to exercise wisdom and discernment in their efforts to be transparent and authentic. Be sure to train your adult leaders concerning what is and what is not appropriate to disclose.

- Your role in teenagers' lives is huge. Embrace the significance and trust God to move through you in ways you can't even imagine.[82]

Here are a few things to consider when you are planning your formal training meetings:

1. **Make them consistent.** As important as it is to meet consistently with your students, it's equally important to meet consistently with your adult volunteers. I (Tim) believe strongly in meeting monthly. In addition to practical training, you have a chance to shepherd your adults and pray for your students. And the synergy that comes out of adult volunteer meetings is significant. One of my former adult volunteers used to tell me that his life was so busy and discouraging, the highlight of his month was the monthly training with our staff. I (Kurt) prefer quarterly meetings largely because we have found our attendance is much higher when we meet less often. Plus, because we are constantly sharing life and meeting informally, a monthly meeting would be overkill. Our friend, Scott Rubin, the junior high worker at Willow Creek, prefers to meet quickly (30 minutes) every single week before their program starts. He feels like his best chance to get everybody in one room at the same time is when they are all already in one room at the same time! Whatever your strategy, pick one and stick with it so your leaders know what is expected.

---

82. I (Tim) like to teach on John 15:5 here, to remind adults that their responsibility is to stay connected to God, and that God does the hard work through us.

2. Make them meaningful. Some of you read "meetings" and cringe. Years ago I (Tim) shared with a mentor my frustration at a leader's lack of attendance at our meetings. His response offended me and challenged me, "Tim, people will come to things that have value to them." As much as I hated to admit it, I knew he was right, and I took the challenge. If I were honest with you, some of the meetings I've led have been real stinkers. But sometimes the Spirit of God becomes tangible and something wonderful happens. In the same way you take seriously your time with students, go the extra mile to prepare a good meeting with your adult volunteers.

3. Make them memorable. Let's play a little game. Let's put ourselves in the place of our adult volunteers for a moment. Think about how many creative, out-of-the-box, "third door"[83] sort of things they've watched us plan and execute for our students. Think about the T-shirts, the backpacks, and the lanyards (man, the lanyards!) they've seen and possibly helped design. Now think about the adult volunteer meetings they've been a part of, in the church building, with sorry food, no excitement, and minimal creativity. Now let's decide to change that! For example, what would happen to your conversation about safety if you held your next meeting at Chuck E. Cheese? (Have you ever noticed their security protocol?)

---

83. "Third door" is a Hollywood term that refers to something the audience would never expect. The first door is what the audience assumes will happen, the second door catches them a little off guard, and the third door is a totally unexpected twist.

How much more would your rock-climbing metaphor stick if you actually went rock climbing (or had your meeting at a rock-climbing wall)? What would your volunteers do if you talked about teamwork over dinner on your way home from a baseball game?[84] You don't have to do something "third door" every time you meet, but creating memorable meetings will increase attendance and effectiveness.

Give honest, loving feedback.

Volunteers deserve to have a clear understanding of what is expected of them. Let people serve where they TILT, constantly expand the box, and let them know in great detail what you're wanting them to accomplish and how you want them to do it. (Can you hear Kurt's voice in the background whispering, "You've got to give people freedom, just not freedom to suck"? If you can, you're as much of a sicko as he is!) Our adult volunteers should never have to guess about what they're doing or how well they are doing it, because we should talk to them about it regularly.

Most people hear a great deal about the things they do wrong and not much about things they do right. We believe we must change that in order to develop confident, competent, and committed leaders. Let's tell our adult volunteers about all the good things they're doing, and let's coach them through the things that need improvement. We should speak truth in love—either one without the other is unhealthy.

---

84. This is not a book about baseball.

Truth without love can be bullish, arrogant, and unkind. Love without truth can be misleading, falsely flattering, and can lead to complacency. Speaking truth in love reminds our adult volunteers that we care about them and want them to do well.

In youth ministry, everything rises and falls on leadership.

For personal reflection:

1. How well do you feel like you are implementing this practice?

      _____ weak

      _____ average

      _____ strong

2. What were some of your "fears" when you first entered youth ministry? How did you overcome them?

3. What are some dangers of allowing leaders to serve where they TILT? What are some rewards?

4. Can you think of any current leaders on your team who may need to have their ministry box expanded?

Experiential option:

Create a "third door" experience for your leaders at your next meeting and do something fun, different, or out of the ordinary.

BEST PRACTICE

CONSISTENTLY VALUE FAMILIES

EYM Marker for a Mature Faith:
The ministry focuses on households, or families

I (Tim) accepted my first paid youth ministry position when I was 19 years old.[85] I was terrified of parents and adults in general. OK, maybe I wasn't terrified, but I had zero interest in meeting with them, talking with them, or leading a training session on parenting with them. I wanted to spend all of my time investing in teenagers, and I wished the parents would just do their thing and let me do mine. Can you relate?

Once I married, my understanding of adult responsibilities grew a bit. I was more aware of the complexities of running a household, and my respect for parents went up a few notches. But part of me still wished the parents would organize themselves and let me minister to their students. Anyone else?

In 2000, my first daughter was born, and the enormity of parenthood hit me in the face like a 95 mph fastball.[86]

---

85. What were they thinking!?!

86. This is not a book about baseball.

Much of what I thought about parents went out the window, and I gained an appreciation for the worrisome questions parents used to ask me about minor details such as hotel arrangements, obedience to the speed limit, and meal choices. I became less irritated with parents' concerns, but still I was less than excited about investing much time in addressing them. They should just let me do my job. Can I get a witness?

Now I have three daughters, and I'm beginning to see occasional flashes of the end of the transition from "my parents are awesome!" to "whatever, dad." As my life changed, I began asking our children's worker the same questions that used to drive me crazy as a young youth worker. And I began relating to youth parents in a way that was new and surprising and enjoyable, as I saw parents take significant steps forward in relationships with their adolescents. Will somebody testify!?!

I predict a time in the near future, when my children are teenagers, where I'll move into another realm of questions. This may be when I call Kurt's wife, Rachel. Despite Kurt's influence, she has managed to raise two teenagers who seem somewhat normal.

There isn't much about parenting teenagers that is easy. Family dynamics are complex, and life is complicated. On one hand it makes sense that youth workers would choose to keep the "youth group world" and the "family world" separate; after all, we can't do everything. It's true, you can't do everything, but the EYM study shows that consistently valuing families and looking for ways to minister with them is something *you can't not do.*

Have you ever been in a meeting or even a casual conversation with youth and/or children's workers when the subject turned to parents? If so, you've probably heard some lamenting (complaining?) about how irresponsible parents are, or how parents expect the church to develop their children spiritually, or how parents just want the church to keep their children out of trouble. These observations may be true, but what if there's another side to this story? What if most parents (85 percent) believed they held the primary responsibility for the spiritual formation of their children? And what if even more parents (96 percent) agreed they were primarily responsible for teaching values to their children? These numbers are taken from a Barna Group report on parents' perspectives.[87]

Surprised? We were, too.

After reading these statistics and talking to parents, we have come to believe that parents are not resistant to being spiritual leaders for their children. In fact, we believe most parents want to embrace their role as the primary spiritual shapers of their children—they just don't know how to do it. And an opportunity just fell into our laps.

Valuing the family is a macro-concept covering a multitude of micro-topics, and we'll do our best to hit on the biggies in this chapter. But in a general sense, valuing the family means showing the same respect and honor for the family that we read in the Bible.

---

87. http://www.barna.org/barna-update/article/5-barna-update/120-parents-accept-responsibility-for-their-childs-spiritual-development-but-struggle-with-effectiveness. Accessed February 21, 2010.

"…you and your children and grandchildren must fear the Lord your God as long as you live. … Listen, O Israel! The Lord is our God, the Lord alone. And you must love the Lord your God with all your heart, all your soul, and all your strength. And you must commit yourselves wholeheartedly to these commands that I am giving you today. Repeat them again and again to your children. Talk about them when you are at home and when you are on the road, when you are going to bed and when you are getting up. Tie them to your hands and wear them on your forehead as reminders. Write them on the doorposts of your house and on your gates" (Deuteronomy 6:2, 4-9 NLT).

Valuing the family means viewing the parent-child relationship as sacred and guarding it appropriately through the things we say (and don't say) and do (and don't do). We believe most (if not all) youth workers value the family and want to nurture family relationships, but sometimes we allow our priorities to be dominated by other important ministry areas. As we discussed in chapter seven, a healthy, balanced youth ministry focuses equally on students, families, and adult volunteers. This distribution makes intuitive sense to most people, but few youth ministries operate in this way.

There are several reasons for this, including:

- Many youth workers are younger and don't feel comfortable ministering to families.

- Ministering to families is an "intangible," and we feel pressure to do things that have tangible results.

- We've tried it before and haven't had the response from parents we had hoped for.

As we explore family-friendly ministry in this chapter, keep this time distribution in mind. Remember, healthy student ministry is balanced across these three areas, and thinking about your ministry to the family is as important as thinking about your ministry to your leaders and your students. And if you want to make the argument that because of the significance of the family it is actually the MOST important thing a youth worker can think about, we won't disagree with you!

So, what are some things you can do to consistently value families?

Be yourself.

We have news for you: You aren't somebody you're not. But other people are! If you are a single, 23-year-old guy who loves sports, don't fret about the fact that you aren't the parent of a teenager. You bring stuff to the table that the families in your church need. If you do happen to be the parent of a teenager, don't fret about the fact that you aren't as young and cool as you once were. You bring stuff to the table that the families in your church need.

Embrace your unique life-stage, figure out how you can uniquely benefit the families in your church, and encourage other adult leaders to do the same thing. Everybody has "gaps" in their abilities to minister to families, but when all the members of your volunteer team view family ministry as a priority and are committed to playing their unique roles, the gaps one person leaves will quickly be filled by somebody else.

Many younger youth workers don't talk to parents about raising children because they feel under-qualified to do so since they have never raised kids of their own. The result is that there is a significant gap in your ministry to parents. One solution might be to simply start your discussion by saying something like, "I have never raised kids on my own, so there is a lot I don't know. But because I spend so much time with teenagers, I do have some things I think you may find interesting." A better solution may be to find somebody in your congregation who has already raised teenagers and empower them to lead the discussion.

Family ministry is a team effort. Be yourself, and let others on the team fill the gaps.

Hey, relational ministry works with parents, too!

Virtually every youth worker would agree that youth ministry that doesn't expand beyond the walls of the church building is ineffective; that's why we so quickly embrace the concept of relational youth ministry. It's funny, then, that very few of us have embraced the idea of fleshing this principle out when it comes to our ministry to parents and the family.

You don't want to become an awkward lurker that shows up uninvited to everything from grandma's birthday party to dad's vasectomy recovery room, but there are some pretty simple things you can do that will help you spend time with families outside the walls of the church. For example:

- When a family is moving, volunteer to help pack boxes.

- When somebody in a family has surgery, ask if you can bring them a meal.

- If a parent gets a promotion, ask if you can take him/her out for a celebratory coffee.

- When a loved one dies, show up at the funeral.

- If you share similar interests or hobbies with a parent, ask if they'd like to participate with you.

- When parents have a skill that you'd like to learn (carpentry, mechanics, art, and so on) ask if they'd be willing to tutor you.

Parents are busy, and their time is scarce. But don't let that keep you from looking for ways to build relationships with them outside the walls of the church.

Provide a little hope and help.

Because every family dynamic is different, there is no one-size-fits-all approach to ministering to parents. But there is one thing every parent needs at some point: hope and help. (OK, maybe those are two things. We like thinking of them together.)

Parents need to have a little hope breathed into them from time to time. They need to know they aren't the only ones who are frustrated with a child's choices. They need to know that it's totally natural for their young teenager to be embarrassed of them. They need to know that dirty rooms, wrinkly shirts, and an aversion to deodorant are all normal for seventh-grade boys, and that staring in the mirror, fussing over hair, and an attraction to makeup are all normal for seventh-grade girls. You won't have an easy answer for every struggle your students' parents are facing, but you can always find a way to share a little hope!

In a similar way, sooner or later every parent is in need of a little help. Instead of feeling the pressure yourself to help out in every scenario, we suggest creating a war chest of "help" you can reach into when needed. Make a list of well-respected adolescent counselors in your area. Also, purchase several parenting books you can loan out, save articles you read and pass them along, and create a short list of websites parents may find helpful.

In my (Kurt) youth group, we are in the process of creating a "been there, done that" ministry that I think has tremendous potential. The idea is to create a database of parents who would be willing to meet with other parents who may need some encouragement in a specific area. For instance, if a teenager is struggling to make acceptable grades, his/her parents would be able to meet with another parent who has already successfully navigated those waters. Our hope is that no matter the issue, we will be able to connect struggling families with others who have already "been there, done that."

One of the most strategic areas to provide a little hope and help is in parents' efforts to disciple their children. This starts by encouraging parents to grow in their own faith, so their teenagers can see God's active presence in their parents' lives. Additionally, youth ministries could provide resources for parents that help them become more intentional about the spiritual formation of their students.[88] Most parents want to help their children grow; they're just not sure how to do it. You can be the one to provide hope and help.

Remember, every family has a different flavor.

Wouldn't it be easy if every family consisted of a mom, a dad, two children, a dog, and a minivan? Simple and boring! Yet even if that were the case, no two families would be the same. Each family has its own distinct flavor. Here are a few ideas to help you minister to some of the more common types of families found in a typical church body.

Nuclear families. I (Tim) served with a pastor once who had a very healthy family (surprising, I know). He and his wife loved one another well, their kids were growing Christ-followers, and they generally seemed to be doing things right. I didn't know what to do. I had no problem coming alongside hurting, dysfunctional families who had deep needs, but I didn't know how to minister to healthy families who didn't really need me. I liked hanging out with them, and I learned a good bit about parenting by watching them, but I often wondered if I did anything to encourage or equip them in their family's journey.

Even families who really do seem to be functioning well need hope and help.

---

88. The Barna Group released a book from their aforementioned research entitled *Revolutionary Parenting* (2007). And have we mentioned the Search Institute? (www.search-institute.org)

Don't neglect the healthy families; in fact, they may be healthy because they are open to input and coaching and would welcome the opportunity to spend time with you.

Single-parent families. Single-parent families are no longer an exception in youth ministry, and students in single-parent homes face unique struggles that flow out of their family makeup:

- Instead of seeing healthy examples of both genders, children in single-parent homes must learn about the gender of the absent parent from other sources. Popular media are broadcasting a message that rarely is healthy. Your congregation can provide a healthy model of both genders.

- Even though most youth workers aren't trained counselors, it's wise to recognize the issues associated with teenagers in single parent homes. A central issue is abandonment. The nature of ministry is that you can't guarantee that you'll be in one location forever, so look for other adults with deep roots in your congregation to build relationships with students in single-parent families.

- Single parents are often living on tight budgets and are often under-employed. Be aware of this when planning activities, and if possible, make scholarships available, even for the fun stuff.

- Even though they are not alone, teenagers in single-parent families sometimes feel awkward because they are missing one parent.[89] Instead of father/son outings, have "dude" outings and provide additional men for students with absentee fathers. Create similar activities for girls.

Blended families. In addition to single-parent families, blended families are becoming a significant percentage of families in the U.S.[90] There are some similarities in ministering to single-parent families and blended families. Some additional ministry opportunities to be aware of include the following:

- Students from blended families often can only attend weekend activities every other week due to custody issues. Be sensitive to how you talk about attendance, commitment to the group, and so on. Many of these students would love to be with your group every weekend if they could, and their spotty attendance isn't a reflection of their commitment, but of their family dynamic.

- Many teenagers in blended families have a difficult time building healthy relationships with their stepparents. This is especially true if the divorce and/or remarriage happened recently. Look for ways to help your students navigate these new relationships. Also, don't be afraid to reach out to the stepparents to give them a little hope and help as they try to "parent" a stepchild.

89. David Elkind coined the phrase "personal fable" to express the over differentiation adolescents sometimes make about their circumstances with respect to other teenagers. In youth ministry terms, it means they think only bad (or good) stuff happens to them.

90. http://www.helpguide.org/mental/blended_families_stepfamilies.htm. Accessed March 9, 2010.

- As teenagers get older, they typically are allowed more freedom in choosing which family they spend time with. Because older teenagers are so busy with school, sports, work, and other commitments, parents often find themselves scrambling to get quality time together. The result is often a great amount of pressure and guilt from both sets of parents as they vie for time.

Families in crisis. Ministering to families in crisis is an entirely different animal. Often youth workers see crises as opportunities for spiritual growth—and we agree. But in the midst of a catastrophe, families need love and support first and spiritual direction later. If a parent calls to tell you her teenager's grandmother just died, don't ask if the grandmother was a Christ-follower. If a teenager calls and confesses to you that she's pregnant, don't ask her if she knew fornication was a sin. Be generous with grace in the midst of crisis, and trust God's Spirit to lead you to deeper spiritual conversations later.

Flood them with information.

One of the central complaints youth workers hear from parents is the lack of good communication between the youth ministry and the family. Often, this is in spite of good intentions and significant effort on the part of the youth worker. And sometimes we just drop the ball. Some youth workers have a communication system that works for them, but it's not meeting the communication needs of the families in the youth ministry. Instead of settling for one form of communication, bombard families with information; heap coals of communication fire on the heads of unsuspecting parents. Spam them details about youth ministry events.

Here are some tried-and-true options:

Parents' meetings. Parents' meetings are still a great opportunity to connect with families. We have the same complaints you do: Not enough parents show up, the ones who really need to be there rarely attend, and those who do attend are usually already on board with everything you are about to discuss! That may all be true, but before you give up entirely on the concept of parent meetings, here are a few reasons we think they still have a place in your ministry:

- Face-to-face communication is always better than phone, e-mail, Facebook™, text messaging, Twitter™, or smoke signals. People don't read e-mails thoroughly, text messaging is limited to 160 characters per text, and not everyone is as tech-savvy as you are.

- You can cast vision, share stories, and encourage and inspire parents way better in a meeting. It's hard to cast vision in an e-mail. When parents hear your voice and watch you speak, they can sense your passion for healthy student ministry. Plus, emotion and passion can be communicated more clearly when you're looking eye-to-eye with someone.

- Momentum is often won or lost in your group meetings. One of your tasks as a leader is to manage the emotional energy of youth ministry in your congregation.[91] If there are rumblings of discontent, an e-mail isn't going to address it. A group meeting will allow you to steer your ministry back on the right track or build on the positive momentum you already have.

A final thought about parent meetings: Go back and read the section about training meetings in chapter seven. Perhaps some of those wonderful and astute insights also apply to parent meetings.

Electronic communication. A while back, I (Tim) got in the habit of sending out a weekly(ish) e-mail newsletter to parents. The newsletter wasn't complicated or long. I typically included a brief devotional thought, a few book or website recommendations, a link to an article on parenting, any pertinent announcements, and a few words of encouragement inviting parents to call me if they ever needed me. Honestly, it's a pain to put it together every week, but one of the reasons I send it out so frequently is to make it easy for parents to get in touch with me; instead of looking for my phone number or e-mail address, they just hit the "reply" button.

You can use also use Facebook™, Twitter™, text messaging, and whatever the latest social networking trend is to barrage parents with important information.

One-on-one conferences. I (Kurt) may be one of the few fathers in America who looks forward to parent/teacher conferences. Part of it is

---

91. Tony Schwartz and Jim Loehr discuss emotional energy and organizational energy *in The Power of Full Engagement* (Free Press, 2005). We're not talking about new age stuff, but momentum and synergy.

because I enjoy getting to know my kids' teachers a little bit better, but it's mostly because I absolutely love hearing other adults' perspectives about my children. They see things in my kids I don't, and they watch them interact in ways I can't. In parent/teacher conferences my children are the sole topic of discussion for 30 minutes. We talk about their strengths, their weaknesses, their successes, and their failures. We figure out ways to work together and keep one another "in the loop" concerning progress we agree needs to be made. (It's true—one time a teacher actually suggested my son had room for improvement.) The part I like best is when the teachers start bragging on my kids, talking about how smart they are, what a joy they are to have in class, how well they behave, and other things parents just love to be told. I'm sure half of it is made up, but it sure is nice to hear!

If schools encourage one-on-one conferences between teachers and parents, why can't churches devise a similar system? How powerful would it be to schedule an occasional parent/youth worker conference! An easy way to do this would be through your small group system. If you have small groups, encourage your small group leaders to try to get 30 minutes with each student's parents once during the school year.

A couple of years ago I (Kurt) gave parents a chance to sign up for "Coffee with Kurt." Most parents didn't take me up on my offer, but the ones who did found it to be an encouraging experience. And so did I.

Guard against accidentally undermining parents.

As we've mentioned a few times, our bias is that youth ministry in general is good, and it has room to improve. Likewise, youth workers in general are good, and they also have room to improve. We personally don't know any youth workers who are intentionally acting like boneheads; we make mistakes, but they're mistakes. So when we write "guard against accidentally undermining parents," we are acknowledging that most parental undermining is inadvertent. But even unintended undermining is hurtful and unhealthy.

One of my (Kurt) repeated themes with my adult volunteers is "Never put a wedge between students and parents." That may seem elementary, so let us give you some tangible examples of things that might unintentionally create friction between parents and teenagers.

- If you tell students that you're showing a PG-13 movie at next weekend's movie night and they need to get a form signed by their parents giving them permission to watch it, you're driving a wedge between students and parents if the parents have told their teenager he/she isn't allowed to watch PG-13 movies.

- If a teenager sits in your office and tells you something his or her parent did, and you reply, "You're right, your dad is wrong," you're driving a wedge between students and parents.

- When you boldly proclaim that parents shouldn't make their child wait until age 16 to date because that is a silly, arbitrary age that doesn't indicate anything, you're driving a wedge between students and the parents who have set that as the age they can begin dating.

I (Kurt) am guilty of unintentionally driving a wedge between students and parents on numerous occasions. The most memorable is the time I made some joke in my lesson about junior highers who still believe in Santa Claus. About two hours after church I got a phone call from the irate parent of a seventh-grade girl who, at least until she went to youth group, still believed in Santa. She made sure I knew that revealing the true identity of Old Saint Nick was not my role. Everything in me wanted to holler back: "Are you kidding me? I did your sheltered little daughter a favor! Don't blame me for the fact that you have been lying to her for far too long. You're really not upset that she found out the truth; you're just embarrassed that you got caught in a lie!" Yep, that's what I wanted to say. And I almost did. But I suddenly realized that even though I didn't agree with this mom's Santa-revealing strategy (or lack thereof), it truly wasn't my role to determine the timing for her. I had unintentionally driven a wedge between a mom and her daughter. I was lucky the mom didn't intentionally drive a stake through my temple!

Respect family time in your programming.

How did we get to this point? Where did we buy into the notion that the best way to develop a lasting faith in Christ is to keep teenagers away from their families and involved in youth group activities as often as possible? It's not unusual for a youth group to meet together on Sunday morning for Sunday school, again on Sunday night for "youth night," again on Wednesday night for small groups, once a month for student leadership, once a month for ministry team training, once a month for

"Freaky Friday Fun Fest," and add to this schedule a few overnighters, a camp or two, and several service projects, and you have a somewhat accurate picture of a typical youth group. Now let's mix in some sports, some school projects, and a part-time job. Is it any wonder our families are frazzled and frantically trying to fit everything in? Is it possible our efforts to provide an attractive youth ministry are actually doing more harm than good?

Time is an expensive commodity in our world today. We are not youth workers who believe students should always choose church activities over non-church activities, but we do believe it is important to have honest conversations with families about priorities, choices, and commitments. The problem is, youth ministry is often a primary contributor to the confusion over priorities, choices, and commitments!

If we claim our youth ministries value families, we must demonstrate that in our activities. Are we asking teenagers to be a part of so many church activities that they have no time to connect with their families? Have we created a culture in our youth ministries that values time spent with the youth group over time spent with families? Are we asking families to fund so many activities that we've overtaxed their budgets? If we claim we value families, we should reflect that in our programming.

Our youth ministries are only as strong as the families we serve. Healthy youth ministries want to help the family win. Maybe part of our solution means doing less youth ministry stuff and helping families do more family stuff.

One simple idea is to create several lists that families can work their way through together:

- 10 movies every family should watch

- 10 board games every family should play

- 5 great day hikes in our community

- 10 cheap family dates for under 10 bucks

Families are a big deal, and one of the best ways to minister to students is to continuously look for ways to consistently value and strengthen the family in which they find themselves.

For personal reflection:

1. How well do you feel like you are implementing this practice?

_____ weak

_____ average

_____ strong

2. What are some things about your current life-stage that may help you minister to families?

3. Jot down the name of the first student who comes to mind. What can you do to provide a little hope and help to his/her parents?

4. In what ways might you be unintentionally driving a wedge between students and parents?

Experiential option:

We hope you will take us up on this one! Consider meeting with your supervisor or senior pastor to discuss the possibility of cutting back some of your youth ministry activities with the purposeful goal of helping families spend more quality time together.

CREATE CONTEXTUALIZED PROGRAMS AND EVENTS

EYM Marker for a Mature Faith:

The ministry establishes "common effective youth ministry practices" and implements custom-designed, integrated approaches to youth ministry

Let's play a quick game of word association. What comes to mind and what emotions are elicited when you hear the word "programs"? It's a dangerous game because for some youth workers, just hearing that word uttered causes a severe rise in blood pressure. In fact, some of you would embrace puppies being kicked or a relaxation of child-labor laws more quickly than you would embrace the idea that programs are an integral part of a healthy youth ministry.

We've heard them all:

- "Programs get in the way of authentic relationships."

- "Programs are a luxury of mega-churches with mega-budgets."

- "Programs only serve to attract a large, shallow crowd."

- "Programs are part of youth ministry 2.0 and are no longer relevant."

- "Today's students hate programs."

- "Programs caused the H1N1 outbreak of '09."

But what if programs aren't so bad after all? Yes, we are glad this is the final chapter of the book, because for some of you, our proposal that programs may not be a tool of Satan would have caused you to put the book down much earlier. You can put it down now, of course, but at least you have already read most of it!

For the sake of this discussion, we'd like to give you our working definition of youth ministry programs. This certainly isn't the only definition and it may not be your definition, but knowing how we define programs will help you as we navigate the topic together. Remember, we have a combined total of over 30 years of youth ministry experience, and Tim has his Ph.D. in youth ministry, so this is a very well thought-out, deep, and profound definition. In fact, it's both a definition and a formula! Are you ready?

PROGRAMS = THE STUFF YOU DO.

By this definition, everything your ministry does is, in essence, a program.

- A big, loud, high-energy Friday night outreach with crazy games and a charismatic guest speaker that attracts hundreds of teenagers? *Program.*

- Spending one-on-one time with students in a coffee shop talking about life? *Program.*

- Taking your youth group on an overseas mission experience? *Program.*

- Refusing to have programs and simply allowing caring adults to spend time with students and join their journey of faith? *Program.* (That is just an organic, non-program-y approach to your youth ministry program!)

In our conversations with youth workers around the country, we've learned that much of the opposition to programs isn't an opposition to doing stuff as a ministry, but rather an opposition to so much of the stuff youth ministry does. Without question, a lot of what youth ministry does is problematic! And as a result, "programs" have gotten a bad rap, and many people have thrown the baby out with the bathwater.

Not too long ago, I (Kurt) was speaking at a youth ministry training event. During one of the breaks, a handful of us decided to grab a coffee together (I'm not a coffee drinker and prefer hot tea or steamed milk… sissy, I know) and continue our discussion. As we drank our coffees and steamed milk with a touch of vanilla, the conversation inevitably turned to sharing with each other some of the stuff our ministries were doing. One of the younger guys spent a few minutes talking about his ministry, and it was obvious that good stuff was happening: His discipleship class was taking students to deeper levels than ever before, they had a surprisingly large number of kids serving on ministry teams, and their "core" kids had suddenly started inviting tons of their pre-Christian friends to their midweek study. At some point, I enthusiastically interrupted and said, "Dude, it sounds like your ministry has some amazing programs!" His response was something like, "First, you have a milk mustache, and second, I don't believe in programs. I don't think God is into programs; he's into us loving students." Initially, the arrogance of his statement caught me and my milk mustache off guard, and I almost said some things I would have regretted. But it quickly dawned on me that my young youth worker friend wasn't being arrogant; we just had different definitions of "programs." It was mostly a semantics issue. When I asked him what he would call those wonderful things his youth ministry was doing he simply said, "I don't know, really. It's just the stuff that seems to work for us right now."

So for the sake of discussion in this chapter, let's assume that almost every youth group in existence is doing something; there is some stuff happening for your students. It may not be big stuff or expensive stuff or flashy stuff or overly organized stuff or even impressive stuff, but there is stuff nonetheless. Some of you may look at your youth group and have the same response my friend had in the coffee shop: "It's just the stuff that seems to work for us right now." Call them what you want: things, stuff, initiatives, activities, or even (wait for it) programs, but they exist and they aren't evil. The truth of the matter is that doing stuff that works for you right now in your church context is a youth ministry best practice identified in the EYM study. Creating contextualized programs ("stuff that seems to work for us right now") for your students to be involved in will help ensure they continue to mature in their faith and stay involved with a local church community after they graduate from high school.

If programs are simply "the stuff you do," the question youth workers have been asking since the beginning of time (or at least since the beginning of youth ministry) is, "How do I decide what stuff to do?" Before we help you answer that question, we want to point out that we made sure this chapter was last (the nine practices aren't meant to be in any particular order of importance) because if you decide the previous eight practices are worth pursuing in your youth ministry setting, the "How do I decide what stuff to do?" question becomes a very easy one to answer.

We've never met a church with an organized youth group that didn't expect said youth group to be doing stuff. The problem is, most of the time they really don't care what you are doing. Very few senior pastors, parents, elders, deacons, CE directors, janitors, and whoever else you ultimately answer to, ever think to ask about the reasoning behind the stuff you choose to do. They just want to make sure you are doing stuff—and lots of it. Our hope is that some of these "non-youth worker" church leaders will read this book (you may need to be the one to put it in their hands) so more of you will be freed of the myth that good youth ministry is a busy ministry doing lots of stuff that doesn't leave a mess (the janitor asked us to throw that part in there). We hope this myth is replaced with an understanding and appreciation of the truth that healthy youth ministry is more important than big, flashy, youth ministry, and healthy youth ministry has the best chance of showing up in a church that embraces the nine best practices.

Back to the "How do I decide what stuff to do?" question, the one we said is very easy to answer. Our answer is best practice nine: Do stuff that helps you accomplish the other eight. That's it? Yep, that's it.

Throughout this book, we've given you a little bit of insight into each of these best practices, but we've tried to avoid telling you how to flesh them out in your setting. In fact, if you dig into the EYM study (and we hope you do), you will discover that among the churches studied, there was much diversity in how the best practices were being implemented; churches were doing all sorts of different stuff (had created all sorts of different programs) that seemed to work in their particular setting.

As you begin to think about your youth ministry and the type of "stuff" you want to do, you may want to consider a few things.

Start with the end in mind.

What do you want to see accomplished in your youth ministry? Why does your youth ministry exist? We hope that after reading this book, the answer to these questions has something to do with the best practices we've discussed! When you know the direction you want your youth ministry to take, it becomes much, much easier to decide what stuff you want to do. You are no longer distracted by whims, ministry trends, and the personal agendas of other people who constantly try to get you to do the stuff they think is most important. (The missions pastor who wants to use your students to smuggle Bibles into China; the Amway sales rep who promises a 20 percent cut if your students sell 100 cases of super cleaner; the over-pushy mom who insists you need to start a Saturday morning "Bible Olympics" ministry…we could do this all day.) Instead you focus on and make decisions according to your already determined end goal.

Think "context," not "cookie cutter."

When thinking about programs, it's tempting to look over the landscape, identify the churches that seem to have successful youth ministries and create a "mini-me" version of their programs in your church. Apparently a whole lot of youth workers are giving into this temptation, because the "What are they doing, and how can I do it, too?" mentality is pandemic. What's most interesting about this phenomenon is the fact that most of us assume that a bigger youth ministry is a better youth ministry, and we should long for and emulate larger youth ministries. We don't pick up the phone and call the smaller, less elaborate youth ministry down the road to see what they are doing—what could we possibly learn from them? Instead we call a much larger church, with a bigger budget, with fancier lights, in a larger city, ministering to a completely different demographic, in hopes that they will be willing to share their silver bullet with us. They don't have a silver bullet, and if they did, it wouldn't fit in your gun, anyway.

Every church is unique—even churches of the same size, in the same town, and of the same tradition. The wise leader understands the context in which he or she is leading, and instead of trying to force somebody else's programs into their setting, this person creates youth ministry programs that are put in place specifically for these students, in this church, in that part of town, from this tradition.

Learn from other churches.

While your context is unique and you should avoid a cookie-cutter approach to programming, it would be foolish to deny the fact that we can learn from each other. Building a youth ministry in a vacuum, void of outside influence, doesn't make much sense. Back in the old days when information traveled much more slowly, youth workers probably had to work much harder to network with each other and share ideas. Rumor has it that when Paul Revere rode his horse through the countryside, he was actually shouting, "The British are coming, the British are coming! And does anybody have a fun game to play with my eighth-graders this Wednesday night?" Luckily times have changed, and youth ministry jokes have gotten better. The world is small, and you have a wealth of information, ideas, and input literally at your fingertips.

In order to avoid the temptation of taking stuff you find online, in resources (this book included), and in conversations with youth workers from other churches and using them in a cookie-cutter way, we suggest asking yourself a few simple questions when you come across a fantastic new idea.

- Would this work exactly "as is" in my context?

- What minor or major tweaks would I need to make in order for it to work in my setting?

- What things in my context would hinder this from being effective? (Space, budget, enough adult leaders, church culture, and other factors.)

- Is the payoff worth the investment? In other words, is the idea so good that the work it would take to customize it to my setting would be offset by great results?

- Will I lose the trust of parents and church leaders or get fired if I do this at my church? I (Kurt) have a ton of freedom, and having been at my church since 1997, I can try just about anything. You may not have the same luxury.

- If I can't (or don't want to) borrow this idea, are there any big-picture principles I can learn from it and apply to something I do want to do?

Become a liquid leader.

I (Kurt) love the phrase "liquid leadership."[92] It reminds me that change is constant and that most of the time, it is a force for good. My role as a leader is to embrace it. Liquid leaders are capable of navigating the times in which they lead, the culture they find themselves in, and the myriad of ever-changing factors influencing that which they lead. Liquid leaders hold tightly to the things that matter but let other things ebb and flow.

Creating programs (doing stuff) in your local context in such a way that allows the other eight practices to manifest requires you to be a liquid leader. You no longer have the luxury of doing things just for the sake of doing them, or doing things simply because students seem to like them, or doing things because…well, because you've always done those things!

---

92. We're not sure exactly who coined this phrase, but Kurt insists it was him. But he also insists he started the "pegging" your jeans trend of the mid-'80s as well as the phrase "cheesy."

When you discover a current program in your youth ministry not reflecting one of the best practices, it will take liquid leadership to know how to address the issue. It will take liquid leadership because how you address that particular program will be different from how you address the next one.

Join forces.

You don't have to do everything on your own, and you can't. Look for strategic ways to partner with other youth groups in your area in order to maximize and multiply your efforts. Having a kingdom mindset makes this easier because you can get excited about the big picture of how God is at work throughout the various churches in your community and the role your group can play. If you are arrogant ("I don't need to partner; we are better off on our own."), insecure ("I don't want to partner; what if my students like the other groups better?"), or afraid ("I don't want to partner; what if my students are exposed to other traditions?"), you will choose not to take advantage of the amazing opportunities offered when you join forces with other youth groups.

A few years ago my (Kurt) friend decided he wanted to kick off the school year by having a big event at his church that would help get students fired up about the year to come. He named it "Fusion" and eagerly invited all the other nearby youth groups to join. He had often heard his students saying that they didn't know other Christians on their campuses and that it was hard to live as a Christ-follower when they felt so outnumbered. "Fusion" was his attempt to bring youth groups together to show that in reality, every campus in their community had lots of kids who loved Jesus and were trying to follow his ways. Today, "Fusion" is a community-wide tradition that attracts more than 1,000 students each year from a variety of churches. Amazing things can happen when you join forces.

Keep it simple.

Back in the day I (Kurt) needed an entire notebook full of charts and graphs to describe our youth ministry programs. If a parent, potential volunteer, or neighboring youth worker wanted to know about our ministry, I would pull out the notebook and say, "I'm glad you asked. Let's start with page one." It was impressive, but I found that nobody was as impressed with it as I was! It was overwhelming, and very few people had the patience to sift through all the information. Today if you want to know about the ministry I lead, I can explain it to you over a cup of something hot on a couple sides of a paper napkin—the world's largest paper napkin! Seriously, any size paper napkin will do. On one side I will write out what we are trying to do, and on the other side I will draw two simple pictures that illustrate how we hope to do it. Of course there's a little more to it than that, and I still have a notebook full of details, but I have learned the power of simplicity.

On the next page, you will see what my napkin art looks like. The front of the napkin shows the three primary areas of emphasis (our three-legged stool) and the back of the napkin shows how we flesh out our ministry to students. If you want more details you will have treat me to lunch!

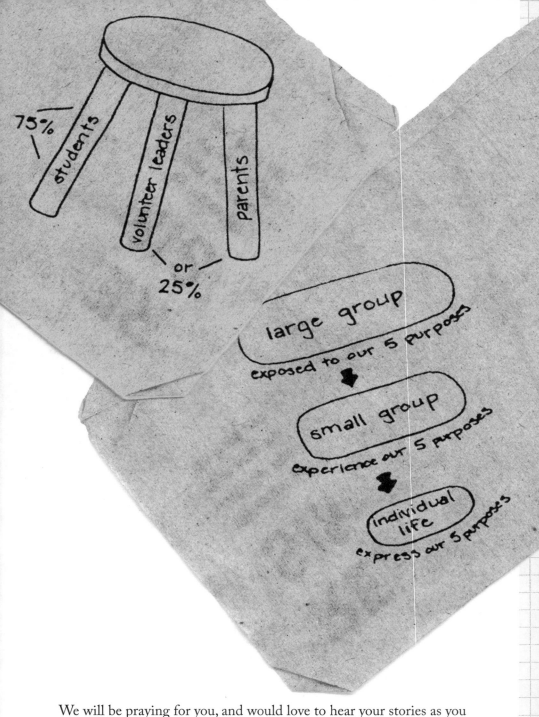

We will be praying for you, and would love to hear your stories as you consider what The 9 Best Practices might look like in your youth ministry.

Thank you for investing into the lives of teenagers; you truly are making a difference. Some might even say you are hitting a homerun for the cause of the kingdom, but this is not a book about baseball.[93]

For personal reflection:

1. How well do you feel like you are implementing this practice?

_____ weak

_____ average

_____ strong

2. Make a list of all "the stuff" your youth ministry does. In what way does each program enhance or hinder the best practices?

3. Of the nine best practices, which ones are you already doing well? Which ones may require some extra attention?

---

93. Goofy to end the book with the same line we used to start it? Probably. Especially since it's not a book about baseball.

4. Is there a youth worker from another church in your area you can pass this book along to? Better yet, is there a youth worker from another church in your area who may want to purchase several dozen? That last part is a joke…no it's not…yes it is, sort of.

Experiential option:

Grab a napkin (grab several, it may take a while) and practice the art of simplicity by trying to articulate the details of your youth ministry in a way that is easily understood.

APPENDIX

AN OVERVIEW OF THE STUDY OF EXEMPLARY CONGREGATIONS IN YOUTH MINISTRY

(... or "Where did this stuff come from, anyway?")

The Study of Exemplary Congregations in Youth Ministry (EYM), funded by Lilly Endowment, Inc., was conducted from 2001-2005 and led by leaders in student ministry from seven major church bodies in the United States: the Assemblies of God, the Catholic Church in America, the Evangelical Covenant Church, the Evangelical Lutheran Church of America, the Presbyterian Church USA, the Southern Baptist Convention, and the United Methodist Church. These leaders had observed a dramatic drop in the percentage of teenagers and young adults who were involved in church communities and ministry. These leaders also observed that some church communities were effective at establishing faith in the lives of students. The ultimate goal of EYM was to identify, via both quantitative and qualitative methodologies, the common factors that typify church communities that were effectively nurturing students' faith.

The EYM researchers developed forty-four faith assets to report the study results. For the purposes of this book, we focused on eight of the main principles that provide insight into all forty-four faith assets.

Using the criteria outlined in chapter one, the seven major church bodies identified church communities that were doing exemplary ministry with students within their respective domains. For the quantitative analysis, data from these exemplary church communities was compared with general church data collected from numerous previous studies secured from the American Religion Data Archive. For the qualitative analysis, data collected from these exemplary church communities was codified and indexed to identify thematic similarities among the exemplary churches.

The quantitative dimension of the study was executed via surveys ranging from 301 to 354 items distributed to four population sets: lead pastors and student workers, paid and volunteer adult youth workers, parents of students, and students. Data was collected from 5,793 surveys from 131 church communities. The qualitative dimension of the study was executed via intensive on-site interviews with seven population sets within a diverse subset of 21 of the 131 above-mentioned church communities: lead pastors, youth workers, other pastoral staff, paid and volunteer adult youth workers, parents of students, older students (ninth-12th grades), and younger students (sixth-eighth grades).

For a more in-depth exploration of the EYM study, please visit www.exemplarym.com or check out their self-published title on the study, *The Spirit and Culture of Youth Ministry: Leading Congregations Toward Exemplary Youth Ministry.*